I0002876

Introduction
to the World of Cryptocurrency:
Getting started with Bitcoin

A Comprehensive Step-by-Step Bitcoin Guide

for Beginners

By

Oleh Lesiv

https://newbitcoinuser.com

Introduction to the World of Cryptocurrency: Getting started with Bitcoin

A comprehensive Step-by-Step Bitcoin Guide for Beginners

by Oleh Lesiv

Editor Eoin Finnegan
Proofreader Nikki Crutchley, www.crucialcorrections.co.nz
Cover Design by Oleh Lesiv
Cover Images Getty Images

Edition: 2019

Published and printed by: Blurb Books

ISBN 978-0-473-50425-0 (Softcover)

ISBN 978-0-473-50426-7 (Hardcover)

For more resources, please visit http:// www.newbitcoinuser.com

About the Author

Oleh Lesiv has been a passionate cryptocurrency and Bitcoin enthusiast since 2017, just before the Bitcoin price has reached its all-time high level. He has five years of trading experience in forex and extensive knowledge of cryptocurrency markets. In 2014, he earned his master's degree in finance science and holds an MSc in Finance from Birkbeck, University of London. An academic background, trading experience and cryptocurrency research gave him a solid understanding of cryptocurrency trading and investing.

In 2018, Oleh worked as a business development manager and helped to develop ICO for one of the blockchain-based start-up projects in London,UK. He is also an active member of the crypto community in Auckland, NZ, and founder of cryptocurrency web blog newbitcoinuser.com. As an author of articles and blog posts on Bitcoin and other cryptocurrencies, he shares his knowledge about cryptocurrency and helps to educate crypto beginners.

He has decided to write this book with a vision to spread the word about Bitcoin and enhance community knowledge of cryptocurrency and blockchain technology.

Acknowledgements

This book is the result of the learning process and research on cryptocurrency for the last two years. I believe it is a great way to share gained skills and knowledge about innovative Bitcoin payment network with others and help its community to grow. Being a crypto enthusiast, I have taken this opportunity to express myself in the best possible way and achieve a big milestone in my career development.

Most of all I would like to thank my good friends Ivana Susilo and Dietrich Truchsess for their contribution to the successful completion of this book. The creation of this work could not have been possible without Ivana Susilo, who took a great part in inspiring and motivating me to write the book. I would also like to express my gratitude to a business developer and cheese food industry entrepreneur, and author of *Homemade Venezuelan and Colombian cheese,* Dietrich Truchsess for his sincere guidance and help.

I am deeply grateful to my respected and loved parents who encouraged me and fully supported me throughout the time of my research.

Special thanks to editor Eoin Finnegan and others who have dedicated their time to review and provide feedback on the manuscript. Without their collaborative contribution to this book the end result wouldn't have been achieved.

Table of Contents

In 1999, Professor Milton Friedman, a Nobel Prize winner in economics stated:

'I think the internet is going to be one of the major forces for reducing the role of government. The one thing that's missing but that will soon be developed, is a reliable e-cash.'

Nine years later, Bitcoin was born.

'Bitcoin is one of the most important inventions in all of human history since the Internet. For the first time ever, anyone can send or receive any amount of money with anyone else, anywhere on the planet, conveniently and without restriction. It's the dawn of a better and freer world.'
-Roger Ver, CEO Bitcoin.com

'Bitcoin is exciting because it shows how cheap it can be. Bitcoin is better than currency in that you don't have to be physically in the same place and, of course, for large transactions, currency can get pretty inconvenient.'
-Bill Gates, co-founder of Microsoft, investor and philanthropist

'Well, I think it is working. There may be other currencies like it that may be even better. But in the meantime, there's a big industry around Bitcoin. — People have made fortunes off Bitcoin, some have lost money. It is volatile, but people make money off of volatility too.'

-Richard Branson, founder of Virgin Galactic, and 400+ businesses

'Bitcoin is a remarkable cryptographic achievement... The ability to create something which is not duplicable in the digital world has enormous value...Lots of people will build businesses on top of that.'

-Eric Schmidt, Executive Chairman of Google

Introduction

Explore the world of cryptocurrency like never before

Introduction

Introduction to the world of cryptocurrency: Getting started with Bitcoin is a step-by-step guide which will help you learn and understand the fundamentals of the first digital currency, Bitcoin. This is one of the most comprehensive and easy to understand guide books for beginners who are interested in gaining or enhancing their knowledge about the world of cryptocurrencies.

The basic concepts of cryptocurrency, Bitcoin and its blockchain technology are introduced in this book. This book covers topics about the creator of Bitcoin and its origin since the inception, explains why Bitcoin is better than conventional money and tells us what makes Bitcoin the perfect global currency. Its content also includes detailed material about Bitcoin's technical properties and the mining process.

Additionally, this book explains how to start with Bitcoin and prepares you for investing in alternative cryptocurrencies. Backed by past data research, it covers the full history of Bitcoin's growth patterns and its major price corrections.

This step-by step guide is suitable for readers with any level of knowledge in cryptocurrency be it a beginner or an expert. Don't worry if it is the first time you have come across the terms 'Bitcoin' and 'cryptocurrency'. It is very likely that by the time you finish reading this book, you will have a good understanding about cryptocurrency. Hence, as a beginner, you can easily understand and get started with Bitcoin without having any previous knowledge.

This book is highly recommended to people who would like to start investing in cryptocurrency and create an additional source of income. It also provides suggestions for experienced investors who would like to discover a list of the most promising alternative cryptocurrencies of the future. Finally, readers can extract the highlighted benefits of using an exchange trading platform or a digital crypto wallet.

Why cryptocurrency?

Being the most secure and trusted online payment network, Bitcoin is set to replace traditional money in the future. Many people believe that its underlying blockchain technology will certainly improve the global payment industry and change the financial world. With such a view, interest in Bitcoin and its mainstream adoption have drastically increased in the last few years. Moreover, the whole cryptocurrency industry has expanded globally with many blockchain-related projects and new crypto services being established. Since investing in digital currencies, infrastructure is increasing, a sign that Bitcoin is going to become the universal currency. And as time passes, it is inevitable that everyone will be engaged with cryptocurrency transactions.

Bitcoin and blockchain technology are considered to be creating new opportunities for a future digital economy. An economy where everyone will be able to perform business transactions without relying on a trusted intermediary or any central entity. An economy where 'unbanked' people who never had access to banking facilities will be able to transact directly with others. By having a personal cryptocurrency wallet on your mobile phone, just like a bank account, you will have full control of your own money. Your funds can't be frozen, and transactions are instantaneously validated by the blockchain-based Bitcoin payment network. Therefore, it will play a significant role in our future daily lives.

Moreover, Bitcoin has proven itself as a profitable long-term investment asset which could continue to yield high returns in the future. In the past, the return on investment in Bitcoin has been the highest in comparison to other traditional assets such as stocks, commodities or even gold. Just in 2017 Bitcoin gained 1,300% in value and contributed to the total 1,500,000% percentage growth over the past ten years.

With an ever-increasing number of Bitcoin users across the globe, it becomes essential that we are equipped with knowledge about cryptocurrencies and are well prepared for the modern 'digital money age'. It will certainly help us to adopt to the changing market dynamics and create new investment opportunities.

What are the topics this book covers?

Being new to the cryptocurrency world, it is very important that you first get a fair idea of what cryptocurrency is. Keeping this in mind, the book consists of eleven chapters that focus on building a strong foundation for cryptocurrency knowledge. Thus, this step-by-step guide, in particular, is useful for people who do not have any knowledge about Bitcoin or may have developed incorrect notions about it.

The first chapter of the book explains the concept of cryptocurrency and its key characteristics. It also contains information about the evolution of cryptocurrency markets.

Bitcoin is a digital currency that does not have a physical form and is designed to exchange monetary value through the Internet. Chapter Two tells us everything about Bitcoin and the main reasons why it is the perfect digital currency. Anyone who is interested in Bitcoin must be aware of its underpinning blockchain technology. Blockchain is an innovative technology that makes Bitcoin a decentralized and most secure payment network. A thorough explanation of how Bitcoin and blockchain technology work is included in the Chapter Three. Reference to the main key features of blockchain will help you to understand why it is considered promising technology in the near future.

A remarkable cryptographic achievement, Bitcoin has many advantages over gold and the US dollar. An interesting perspective has been presented in Chapter Four, which explains why Bitcoin will succeed as a store of value.

Would you like to know how new Bitcoins are being created and who maintains the Bitcoin network? Then you should read about the Bitcoin mining process explained in Chapter Five.

The next four chapters introduce you to the world of alternative cryptocurrencies and explain why an Initial Coin Offering could be an excellent investment opportunity for early investors. Here you will learn everything about the types of altcoins and what to consider whilst selecting the right crypto coins for your portfolio. Moreover, in this section of the book, we will discuss the most promising cryptocurrencies that, in my opinion, could have a great potential for growth in the long run. These chapters will help you to develop a good understanding of how to build a diversified and rewarding investment portfolio.

Bitcoin has a very interesting story about the origin and motives behind its creation. Chapter Ten talks about the mysterious developer of Bitcoin, the pseudonymous Satoshi Nakamoto, and offers a glimpse of the mystery surrounding its development.

If the cryptocurrency world excites you but you don't know how to get started with Bitcoin, then read the last chapter of this book. Chapter Eleven will guide you through the 'beginner' steps and explains in detail how to choose and download a secure cryptocurrency wallet, transfer funds and purchase your first Bitcoin. This chapter also tells you about the most popular places you can buy cryptocurrency and how to transfer it to your digital wallet. Furthermore, you will learn how to create an account with a cryptocurrency exchange trading platform and how to start investing in cryptocurrencies.

Embark on an adventure with *Introduction to the world of cryptocurrency: Getting started with Bitcoin* and gain the knowledge that one day will help you to become a successful cryptocurrency investor.

Chapter One

What is cryptocurrency?

Cryptocurrency is such a powerful concept that it can almost overturn governments.

What does cryptocurrency mean?

Cryptocurrency is often referred to as 'digital currency' or 'virtual currency'.

Cryptocurrency is a new kind of internet-based money that only exists digitally or virtually. It is an alternative digital form of payment to cash, credit cards, and other digital money systems such as PayPal or Apple Pay. Cryptocurrencies are designed to work as a medium of exchange for goods and services (just like any traditional currency) and transfer monetary value via the Internet.

This innovative digital payment system uses cryptography techniques and blockchain technology to regulate its generation, control the supply of new units (coins) of a particular cryptocurrency and verify the transfer of funds. Therefore, exchange of digital currencies relies on encryption principles which make transactions very secure.

Cryptography means a form of encryption heavily based on complex mathematical theories and best practices of the computer which is practically infeasible to decrypt. In other words, it is the process of converting text or numbers into a code you can't break. Hence, it secures all cryptocurrency transactions and allows information to be kept secret. Today, cryptography is at the heart of the worldwide communication network.

Blockchain is a global online decentralized database that is shared amongst all computers around the world, but not in one central location. It is the most secure virtual accounting system that underpins cryptocurrency payment networks. Because it exists on the Internet, anyone with an internet connection can use it anywhere in the world.

It may look like the cryptocurrency payment system works in a similar way to traditional digital money. However, there is a significant difference between them. For example, widely used credit cards or PayPal are centralized payment methods of fiat currencies like USD, EUR, GBP or other traditional currencies. The value of fiat currency is regulated and controlled through the process of printing by central banks and governments. Unlike those digital payments, cryptocurrency is not regulated by any bank, government or centralized financial authorities. It relies on the power of transparent and fully decentralized blockchain technology to guarantee its value and confirm transactions. Most cryptocurrencies are designed to decrease in supply of new coins over time which creates an upper limit for the total volume. That is different from fiat currencies, where financial institutions can always create more money, and hence increase the inflation rate.

Network users verify every transaction and those transactions become a matter of public record on the shared digital ledger called blockchain. An entire network of computers have an identical copy of the database and change its records by a common agreement based on pure mathematics. This prevents the same digital currency from being spent twice by the same person. Essentially, cryptocurrencies are limited coded records in a database that no one can change unless specific conditions are fulfilled.

Cryptocurrencies can be transferred directly between people without using an intermediary, like a bank. Most importantly, they were created with the intention to make central banks redundant. Thus, cryptocurrencies operate independently of a central bank and can be exchanged peer to peer, through online cryptocurrency exchanges or brokers. Alternatively, they can be purchased via ATMs or by participating in Initial Coin Offerings.

There have been many attempts at creating a digital currency during the 90s technology boom with digital systems like Bit Gold, DigiCash, B-money, Flooz, Beenz emerging on the market. But none of them were able to solve the double spending problem. The first cryptocurrency to provide a solution for securing digital transactions was Bitcoin back in January 2009. Bitcoin was introduced as an open-source software by a pseudonymous developer under the name Satoshi Nakamoto. The main advantage of Bitcoin is its independence from world governments, banks and corporations. Not one authority can interfere with transactions or take people's money away.

Today, there are over 4,000 cryptocurrencies available in the digital market right now. Ethereum, Litecoin, Dash, EOS, Monero, ZCash and Ripple are other well-known examples of alternative cryptocurrencies. While hundreds of different cryptocurrencies exist, most of them are based on one or two consensus-keeping protocol algorithms: Proof-of-Work and Proof-of-Stake. These strong cryptographic methods are used to confirm transactions on the blockchain network and produce new coins supply.

Initially, Bitcoin was introduced to the world as a first fully decentralized digital payment network. Until today the crypto community is hoping that one day the most leading cryptocurrency will become a widely used form of payment. Gradually, as Bitcoin popularity grows, more and more businesses and merchants from small local shops, bars and restaurants to industry giants are accepting payments in Bitcoin.

However, due to its high volatility and constantly fluctuating prices, it is natural that the spending options for Bitcoin are still limited. Another current difficulty for Bitcoin is the scalability issue. Its underlying blockchain technology is able to process only a few transactions per second. At the moment Bitcoin simply can't scale to compete with payment giants such as Visa or Mastercard.

Despite this you can buy virtually everything with Bitcoin. It became a prime opportunity for a long-term investment – an asset much like gold. Many investors are beginning to see Bitcoin as the best store of value. Whilst cryptocurrencies other than Bitcoin are becoming widely accepted as a viable form of payment.

Being significantly faster and cheaper than Bitcoin, other cryptocurrencies are more convenient for many people and merchants. It's inevitable that in the future a few cryptocurrencies will become global digital currencies used for daily life transactions.

Every day new cryptocurrencies are entering the market with their unique use case and problem-solving techniques. Although they try to differentiate between themselves, most cryptocurrencies have the same characteristics: security, transparency, immutability, global accessibility, speed and price, low transaction fees, ownership, identity protection and risk-free for sellers.

Security: A central bank can change the money supply, an incompetent government can change or lose records or records of ownership can be damaged by water or fire, even if they're stored in digital form. Cryptocurrencies by their nature are decentralized. Records don't exist in one location but in hundreds or thousands of servers around the world.

Transparency: Almost every cryptocurrency is an open source with its source code available for everyone to see and is completely transparent. Thus, it is possible for everyone to see every transaction that has occurred since the cryptocurrency creation.

Immutability: It is impossible to change the transaction history. All the transactions are fully verified and have taken place without the need of approval by any third party.

Global accessibility: You can send or receive cryptocurrency from anywhere in the world. You don't have to be physically in the same place as long as you have access to the Internet. The speed and the cost of the transaction is the same for somebody using mobile or fibre connection.

Speed and price: Usually bank transfers take between 3 and 5 working days and offer low exchange rates between countries. Cryptocurrency transactions times vary from instantaneous to one hour and there is no need to exchange currency.

Low transaction fees: The amount sent will be the amount received with small or almost zero transaction fees. Because miners are rewarded cryptocurrency from the network itself, there are typically little to no fees for transactions.

Ownership: You are the only holder of your digital private key. Unlike funds stored at the bank, your cryptocurrency cannot be frozen or limited by any financial or government institution.

Identity protection: Cryptocurrency can be sent directly to a recipient without any information other than the total amount you wish to transfer. Paying with bank cards requires submitting confidential banking information that could be stolen or compromised.

Risk-free for sellers: Cryptocurrency payments can't be reversed, and merchants don't have to worry about stopped payments. The blockchain makes it difficult for you to be defrauded.

Cryptocurrencies and blockchain technology have the potential to change the global economic system. People around the world are slowly coming around to the fact they now have a better alternative to the traditional banking system. Cryptocurrency transactions can be done with minimal processing fees, allowing users to avoid high costs charged by traditional financial institutions. Due to a limited, controlled supply that is not changeable by a government, a bank or any central institution, cryptocurrencies offer a trustworthy monetary policy. It takes away the control that central banks have on the inflation or deflation by manipulating the monetary supply.

Certainly, it is paramount benefit for third-world countries like Venezuela, Colombia or Zimbabwe, where the inflation has soared by thousands of percent. They turn to cryptocurrencies as Bitcoin, Litecoin and Dash seem like good options to protect themselves against the devaluation of their national currency. More and more people are understanding this fundamental difference and accepting the change.

A good thing about cryptocurrencies is that nobody owns them in the sense that it's a democratic arrangement through the distributed ledger we all own, the ownership of the block. Cryptocurrencies soon can become an unavoidable financial element of the Internet. They will certainly revolutionize everything from insurance, logistics and the stock market to ownership and even create entire economies which don't currently exist. There is a lot of information, articles, white papers and tutorials all over the Internet. Spend a few hours per week reading and do thorough research about cryptocurrencies. You need to fully understand what cryptocurrency is and all the risks that are involved prior to investing in Bitcoin.

About cryptocurrency market

The cryptocurrency market is an incredibly dynamic and fast growing market for both investors and traders. Whilst the market is relatively new, most people find it difficult to understand the concept of cryptocurrency itself. The cryptocurrency market is still at the formation stage, which means that cryptocurrency exchange rates have great volatility. The amount you pay or receive one day can be significantly different the next day. Thus, there is still a small number of people and businesses that are accepting cryptocurrencies compared to those using debit and credit card payments. The functioning of the cryptocurrency market is the same as that of some commodities (coffee, gold, etc) that are mined and sold into the markets. The prices of cryptocurrencies are fluctuating as per the demand and supply.

The cryptocurrency market is a complex, interrelated system of small and large private and institutional investors making uncoordinated decisions about a huge variety of investments in cryptocurrency assets. There are many peer-to-peer local crypto markets, exchanges and brokerage services where you can trade Bitcoin for other currencies and make use of price fluctuations to make extra profits.

Today, the cryptocurrency market, with over 4,000 cryptocurrencies, is still a new market at the early stage of its development. It could take some time before various cryptocurrencies will reach their full potential. Therefore, investing in cryptocurrencies could be better in terms of return on investment and quite profitable over time.

Amongst all cryptocurrencies, Bitcoin has become the best performing emerging digital asset class. Over the last ten years, it has outperformed the return on investment of major financial assets such as stocks and shares (S&P, Dow, Nasdaq) during the longest bull run. Although the leading cryptocurrency experienced more than 80% drop during 2018, it has gained more than 450% in the last two years. In comparison, the gains for the S&P 500 and gold were 19.9% and 1.3% respectively.

In 2019, cryptocurrency Bitcoin continues to outperform the traditional stock market and commodities including oil and gold. Consequently, Bitcoin has offered to its investors much higher returns than any other asset class. Many analysts believe that Bitcoin is about to set a new parabolic growth cycle for the next five years. Moreover, it is capable of increasing in value by as much as fifty times and taking its market capitalization to a higher level. Such an increase would bring Bitcoin into the same value class as assets like gold.

Ranging from only a few pennies to a few hundred dollars in price, the combined value of the crypto market is around US$230–$250 billion (at the time of writing this book). The leading cryptocurrency Bitcoin represents slightly more than 67% of the total market value. In December 2017, the total market capitalization of all cryptocurrencies reached the all-time high level of around US$800 billion. Although the cryptocurrency market lost its value by 80% in 2018, it has the tendency to follow an upward trend with the cycles of ups and downs. Thus, it is expected that within the next 3–5 years, the crypto market could reach a value in the trillions of dollars. This is only a small share compared to other global markets such as gold, stocks or shares. By comparison, the total value of all the world's gold is $7.7 trillion, and US stocks are estimated at US$30 trillion. For example, the total market capital valuation of FAANG – five most popular and best-performing technology stocks Facebook (FB), Amazon(AMZN), Apple (AAPL), Netflix (NFLX), and Alphabet Google (GOOG) summed up to US $3.2 trillion.

There is no doubt the cryptocurrency market is still a growing market and has a lot of room to expand. Today, there is an excellent opportunity to select a few promising cryptocurrencies at cheaper price levels and include them in your investment portfolio. In the long run, cryptocurrency investment can lead to comfortable high returns.

Chapter Two

What makes Bitcoin perfect?

Bitcoin is the beginning of something great and is going to change the world. There is so much potential.

What is Bitcoin?

Bitcoin, the most popular cryptocurrency, is often referred to as 'electronic cash' as it doesn't have a physical form. It is a purely decentralized digital currency that can be sent directly in a peer-to-peer way without the involvement of any third party. Therefore, Bitcoin is a secure and trusted innovative payment system of the future. It doesn't require a central bank or single administrative central authority to verify transactions. Thus, elimination of the need for a bank allows people to have full control of their funds. They can freely send money to anyone and anywhere in the world. Furthermore, it is fast, secure and cheap.

With no government authority controlling this network, Bitcoin has managed to gain the trust of many people over the past decade. Many people believe that such unique properties can help Bitcoin to get on the path towards mainstream adoption.

Bitcoin makes it easy to send real money quickly to anywhere in the world and can also be used to make small purchases with a variety of online retailers, pay for property, hotels, flights, jewellery, Apple apps, and services such as university degree fees. Giant companies like Microsoft and Dell accept payments in Bitcoin for a variety of their products and digital content.

It has unique properties such as fast transactions, low processing fees, nobody owns or controls Bitcoin, your account can't be frozen which could not be covered by any previous payment system. Bitcoin is an open-source programmable money, and anyone can review the code. It can be used in any country; its design is public and the issuing of Bitcoins is carried out collectively by the network.

Bitcoin opens up a whole new platform for future innovations and it is changing finance the same way the Web changed publishing and communication. It is a great way for businesses to minimize transaction fees compared to traditional online payment mechanisms. Bitcoin also provides users with a unique trading experience.

Bitcoin has all the characteristics of a digital currency:

Decentralized: Bitcoin was created with freedom in mind. Its main objective was the network's independence from any governing authority controlling the transactions, imposing fees and being in charge of people's money. It is designed so that every person and business, as well as every computer involved in mining and transaction verification, becomes part of a network.

Anonymous: Nowadays banks know almost everything about their clients, including personal identity, phone numbers, credit history and so on. With Bitcoin it is different as the wallet is not linked to any personal identifying information.

Transparent: Every Bitcoin transaction that happened is stored in the blockchain and is completely transparent and visible to everyone.

Fast: The Bitcoin network processes payments almost instantaneously and it takes just a few minutes for someone on the other side of the world to receive the money.

Non-reversible: Once the Bitcoin payment is processed, there is no way of getting your money back, unless the recipient wants to send it back to you. This ensures the reception of payment, meaning that whoever you are trading with can't scam you by claiming that they never got the money.

High portability: Bitcoin is completely digital, which means it should be easy to carry and use, and practically any sum of money could be carried on a USB stick, hardware wallet or stored online.

Safety and control: Bitcoin users are able to control their transactions, and no one can withdraw money from your account without your agreement. Furthermore, their identities and personal information are always protected as it doesn't have to be disclosed to make a payment. Bitcoins do not carry any personal identifying information such as names or physical addresses.

Non-counterfeited: Sometimes in the digital world, the same money is being spent twice, making both transactions fraudulent. Bitcoin, like most other cryptocurrencies, uses blockchain technology as well as the consensus mechanisms built into all Bitcoin algorithms to prevent double spend.

It would be unfair not to mention the current drawbacks of Bitcoin. It is recognized and legal in many countries where its use and trade are encouraged. However, some of the world's governments banned and outlawed Bitcoin as they still don't have any regulations regarding it. At the moment governments and banks are not able to control Bitcoin and it's almost unregulated. As its popularity is growing, law enforcement agencies, tax authorities, legal regulators and governments worldwide will try to understand the concept of cryptocurrencies and take it under control. A regulated and governed Bitcoin will be an absolutely different currency in the future.

The value of Bitcoin is unpredictable and changes rapidly as it is subject to drastic price fluctuations. Bitcoin's high volatility causes its price to skyrocket and then sharply fall, which can cause significant financial damage to an investor. Losing the 'key' – a unique password necessary to access a Bitcoin wallet – means losing your wallet. It is very important for Bitcoin users to store a wallet backup and know how to restore it.

Chapter Three

Bitcoin and the blockchain technology

There is some really good technology in terms of sharing databases and verifying transactions that is talked about as blockchain. That is a good thing.

What is the blockchain technology and how does it work?

The Bitcoin payment network uses blockchain technology which helps to verify all the transactions. It is an incorruptible digital ledger that can be programmed to record not just financial transactions but almost everything of value. The decentralized feature of blockchain enables one internet user to transfer a unique piece of digital property to another internet user in such way that the transaction is guaranteed to be safe, secure and can be seen on the 'block' without permission from anybody.

Bitcoin and blockchain are revolutionary technologies that enable a new way to send payments over the Internet without being linked to a real identity. Furthermore, Bitcoin is transferred directly from person to person across the Internet without going through the traditional banking system or clearing house. It is an open accounting network where thousands of computers all over the world work together to track ownership of digital currency called Bitcoin.

When you send someone Bitcoins, the transaction is broadcast to the entire network. The Bitcoin network is secured by individuals called miners. Miners are rewarded with newly generated Bitcoins for verifying transactions. After the transaction is verified, it's recorded in a transparent public blockchain ledger and synchronized on all decentralized 'nodes' (computers) that are part of the blockchain peer-to-peer network.

All the digital records of transactions are encrypted first and then combined chronologically into the spreadsheet called 'block'. Each block contains a certain number of approved transactions and has its own unique cryptographic number called 'hash'. The hash of each block is added to the next block. It makes data contained within each block extremely tamper resistant and highly secure. The whole family of blocks are connected to each other and form the blockchain. Being an open ledger, the blockchain contains a record of every bitcoin transaction that has occurred since the system began. It is shared and maintained on the network. Everyone has access to the ledger.

Blockchain technology is designed to reduce fraud and corruption and enables secure information sharing online, which makes cryptocurrencies possible. Blockchain is an accounting type diary that updates itself automatically every ten minutes without any central computer instructions. One of the main features of blockchain is immutability. Once the blockchain ledger is updated, it can no longer be changed and thus, it can't be forged. Blockchain creates a shared database, but one that is duplicated millions of times across a network of computers. Most blockchain transactions are publicly viewable and transparent. Every time new transactions are added and an update is made to a blockchain ledger database, it's available and visible to everyone on the network at the same time who has access to it. Since a blockchain database is not controlled by anyone or not stored in a single, centralized location the information it holds is easy to verify and hard to corrupt. This makes all the transactions secure.

Blockchain technology was the first to resolve the issue of double spending without using any centralized authority. Therefore, the same digital coin cannot be used twice and only one of the two transactions will succeed. By allowing distribution of digital information which cannot be copied, blockchain technology created the backbone for a new era of the Internet (Web 3.0). The decentralized blockchain system is going to change lives from the way we transact in business or manage valuable assets, to the way we operate machines, rent a car and even prove who we are.

Key properties of blockchain

The main key features which make blockchain a promising technology of the future:

Decentralized: Rather than relying on a central authority to confirm transactions between users, blockchain utilizes innovative consensus protocol across a decentralized network of computers (nodes). They validate transactions and record data in the public digital ledger that is synchronized on all nodes. Hence, multiple copies of updated blockchain ledger are stored on every computer that is part of the blockchain network. Any changes to the ledger are reflected in all copies in minutes, or in some cases, seconds. Because blockchain doesn't have a central point of control, it allows the users to make an exchange without the intermediation of a third party, thus eliminating risk.

Safe and secure: Blockchain technology uses cryptography tools which means that all the information and transactions are encrypted. The users hold the private keys and control access to their data. Because each transaction has its own unique identification hash key (string of numbers and letters), it prevents double spending.

Moreover, after a transaction has been recorded on the ledger and copied on every computer, no participants can make any changes. It doesn't matter who you are, you just don't have the power to do that. This is because of the need for the computers to give 'proof of work', which involves solving a complex math problem at the odds of 1 in 7 trillion. This ultimately renders any attempts of hacking the system useless.

Additionally, once the transaction is performed and approved, it cannot be reversed. It is practically impossible to edit or change any data that has been recorded on the blockchain.

Lastly, because everyone can have a copy of the blockchain, we can regard it as being distributed; thus, the blockchain itself is not subject to the control of a single entity. This has the added advantage of making the blockchain incredibly secure, as there is not one single point of failure.

Therefore, there is no easy way to hack, destroy or manipulate multiple copies of the blockchain ledger on the network. All transactions are immutable, meaning they cannot be altered or deleted.

Transparent: After all verified transactions are added to the blockchain ledger, it's shared with each party involved, which has its own copy of the entire blockchain. Therefore, the blockchain is made public and everyone has access to the book. What that means is that it is possible to view the user's public address and their holdings and transactions they carried out. Anyone can also see changes that are made to the public blockchain. The only identity of a user remains concealed behind powerful cryptography. This helps to preserve a degree of privacy.

This level of transparency has not existed within a financial system before, especially in regard to large financial institutions. In the past, they were able to use their customers funds without anyone's knowledge and not always in the most honest way. The Global Crisis of 2008 is an example of this issue. Blockchain has the potential to add a degree of accountability and transparency to any business beyond finance that has not existed to date.

High speed & low cost: In comparison to the traditional banking system, blockchain transactions have a much higher transaction rate and can reduce transaction times to only a few minutes. This allows transactions to occur almost instantaneously. They can be processed anytime compared to traditional ways through banks which need a much longer period. As it is a peer-to-peer way of exchange, blockchain eliminates third-party intermediaries and removes overhead costs. Blockchain provides a great opportunity to reduce transaction fees.

Single public ledger: Despite having multiple copies, there is only one ledger for the entire blockchain network. With all transactions being added to a single public ledger, it reduces the clutter and complications of many ledgers. If you need to view or study a particular transaction, there is only one place to go.

The blockchain consists of a large set of rules and specifications that are programmed into it. Those specifications are called protocols, which made blockchain a secured peer-to-peer information database. The blockchain protocols ensure that the network runs autonomously and isn't controlled by anyone.

The blockchain is ideal for 'smart contracts' that define the rules and penalties around a specific agreement in the same way as traditional contracts do. However, the big difference is that smart contracts are protocols coded in a way so that they automatically enforce the performance of a contract by adding the terms of the agreement into the code and are executed once a specific criterion is met. Smart contracts are the best way to exclude any third party from the transaction and make transaction prices lower, as they need no validation. Smart contracts are implemented in most cryptocurrencies to control the transfers of digital currency. They also may be used in voting, management, real estate, medicine and data storage.

Moreover, the blockchain can be used for warranties and insurance claims, financial derivatives, identity verification, archiving and file storage, the protection of intellectual property, crime, elections and polls, and social media. Along the way, it will transform banks and other financial institutions, hospitals, and companies, among others. Today many governments and sectors are exploring ways to implement blockchain technology to improve productivity and accountability. The blockchain economy will provide ample choice and will be a disciplined market and asset-based economy.

The blockchain is a new infrastructure layer of the Internet. It is going to form the basis of new technological innovations and replace what operating systems do. This new technology has the potential to establish trust mechanisms at a much lower cost and might be the key to prevent future financial crises. It is the future of the Internet.

Even Apple's co-founder Steve Wozniak called blockchain 'the next major IT revolution that is about to happen'. He mentioned that both blockchain technology and Bitcoin will reach their full potential in a decade. However, with blockchain technology being widely used by many crypto enthusiasts, acceptance might come sooner. In October 2017, Wozniak said at the Money 20/20 conference in Las Vegas that Bitcoin is a better standard of financial value than gold or the US dollar. He was also enthusiastic about Ethereum and described it as a platform similar to Apple's. Steve Wozniak said that in the long-term Ethereum can become as influential as Apple.

Chapter Four

Why is Bitcoin better than gold or the US dollar?

Bitcoin is the money of the people; fiat currency is the money of the government. The relative success of Bitcoin proves that money first and foremost depends on trust. Neither gold nor bonds are needed to back up a currency.

Why will Bitcoin succeed?

The main advantage of Bitcoin is that it has controlled fixed supply, which is limited and capped at 21 million in total. As of August 2019, Bitcoin has reached a total circulation amount of 18 million coins, which is around 85% of the total amount of Bitcoin that there ever will be in existence. The last Bitcoin should be mined sometime in the year 2140. Unlike the American dollar and British pound (fiat currencies), Bitcoin is not regulated by a single central bank and cannot be corrupted.

Fiat currencies are the world's dominant form of currency today that are entirely controlled in their supply and creation by governments and are backed by nothing but faith in that government. Gold, unlike fiat currencies, requires no faith and trust in a government to manage its money supply in order to believe that it will retain its value over time. This is because gold has no central authority that controls it and effectively dictates its supply and creation.

Gold is fundamentally scarce and only small amounts of it can be mined every year and added to the whole supply. No government, no matter how much they wanted to or needed to, could produce more gold on demand. Fiat currencies can and often have been printed on demand by governments whenever they were short on cash. The process of printing more money generally leads to inflation.

Gold doesn't inflate like fiat currencies do. That is because there is limited supply, and things tend to cost the same in gold over long periods of time. This makes gold, in many ways, a better store of value based on fundamental principles than fiat currencies over time. While gold has proven to be a great store of value over time, it is incredibly poor for actual day-to-day use in today's economy.

To transact with gold is very inconvenient and it is time consuming to send gold to anyone who isn't in the same location. For these reasons fiat currencies have been preferred for everyday use. Bitcoin, however, with the help of recent technologies solves all these issues as it incorporates all of the best elements of gold – its inherent scarcity and decentralized nature – and then solves all the shortcomings of gold, in allowing it to be globally transactable extremely quickly.

Gold is physically mined out of the ground whilst Bitcoin is 'mined' digitally. However, the production of Bitcoin is controlled by code that dictates that a specific solution to a given problem must be found in order to unlock new Bitcoins. This system has many advantages over gold's natural system of being mined out of the ground. Gold mining is effectively random and not dictated by any computer algorithm and is much more unpredictable in its output at any given moment of time. Bitcoin, on the other hand, will always be mined on a perfectly regulated schedule, because it can adapt no matter how many people mine it or how Bitcoin mining hardware advances.

Executive chairman of Google Eric Schmidt said: 'Bitcoin is a remarkable cryptographic achievement. The ability to create something, which is not duplicable in the digital world has enormous value. Lots of people will build business on top of that.'

Richard Branson, founder of Virgin Galactic and more than 400 other businesses: 'Well, I think it is working. There may be other currencies like it that may be even better. But in the meantime, there is a big industry around Bitcoin.'

Bill Gates, co-founder of Microsoft, investor and philanthropist said that Bitcoin is better than currency in that you don't have to be physically in the same place and, of course, for large transactions, currency can get pretty inconvenient.

Bitcoin has the potential to grow up to forty times its current value, according to cryptocurrency billionaire Cameron Winklevoss, who also described the leading digital currency as 'better than gold'.

Chapter Five

Bitcoin and the mining process

I think the fact that within the Bitcoin universe an algorithm replaces the functions of the government ... is actually pretty cool.

About the Bitcoin network

There are no physical Bitcoins and they cannot be printed. A Bitcoin is represented by the record of its transactions between different addresses and the balances, which are both kept on a public ledger in the cloud. Addresses consist of randomly generated sequences of letters and numbers linked through the mathematical encryption algorithm that was used to create them. They are often called public or private 'keys'. The public key, comparable to a bank account number, serves as the address, which is published to the world and to which others may send Bitcoins. The private key, comparable to an ATM PIN, is meant to be kept in secret, and only used to authorize Bitcoin transmissions. Bitcoins do not carry any personal identifying information such as names or physical addresses. Bitcoins are broken down to eight decimal places, and this smallest unit is referred to as a 'satoshi'. The best way to explain this is that Bitcoins are like dollars and satoshi are like cents.

Earlier in this book I have briefly mentioned Bitcoin mining and miners. Now I am going to explain in detail to you what the Bitcoin mining process is and who the miners are, so you have a good understanding how the Bitcoin network operates.

When Satoshi released his Bitcoin software, he intended it to be mined on ordinary computer CPUs. At the very beginning, early adopters and computer geeks used laptop computers to solve computational problems and secure their first coins. So a few early miners were fortunate enough to mine a large number of Bitcoins before it gained significant value. Perhaps, the most famous of these is the Bitcoin creator, Satoshi Nakamoto. He holds almost one million coins which is equivalent to 4.75% of the total supply.

With time, the mining difficulty of solving mathematical puzzles has been increasing. Thus, miners realized that the only profitable way to mine Bitcoin was by using specialized Bitcoin mining hardware. Today it is a highly specialized industry with the concentration of mining power in the hands of a few companies. Therefore, most Bitcoin mining is done by enterprises on a large scale in the locations with cheap electricity supply. It seems like at least 50% of mining hardware is located within China. Recently, Canada has also become a leader in crypto mining due to its low energy costs.

What is Bitcoin mining and how does it work?

Bitcoin mining is a process of adding Bitcoin transactions and securing all the records into the public ledger blockchain that is done through the use of computer processing power. After each set of transactions is processed and validated by miners, it is included in a block. The block is secured by miners and very strict cryptographic rules that prevent previous blocks from being modified because doing so would invalidate all following blocks. These specific rules also prevent any individual from easily adding new blocks into the blockchain. Thus, no individual can control what is included in the blockchain, replace parts of the blockchain or attempt re-spending any money that has already been spent somewhere else.

Mining ensures a chronological order in the blockchain and allows different computers to agree on the current state of the system. Every transaction is confirmed to the rest of the network, and every single user of the network can access the ledger. Mining is an important part of Bitcoin and its primary purpose is keeping the Bitcoin network stable, safe and secure.

Where do Bitcoins come from?

Bitcoin mining is also the process through which new Bitcoins are released into circulation. As we already know, all mining activities are carried out by miners. Miners contribute their computing power and use special software to solve difficult mathematical hash problems to confirm transactions. They discover a new block which is chained to the previous block whilst being added to the blockchain ledger.

Because their role is to secure the network and process transactions, as a reward, miners receive a payment in the form of new Bitcoins. The number of Bitcoins awarded to miners depends on the computing power that they contribute to generate new Bitcoins. They get rewards for their service every ten minutes. Furthermore, miners are not solely rewarded by the new Bitcoin that is generated each time they mine a block. They are also awarded 'transaction fees' paid by users for every transaction that they approve. This provides a smart way to issue the currency and also creates an incentive for more people to mine. Miners are the most important part of the Bitcoin network as they are providing a bookkeeping service for the whole Bitcoin community.

Bitcoin mining is designed to be difficult and to control the number of blocks found each day by miners. In 2009 the block reward was 50 new Bitcoins and it decreases at regular intervals. As of October 2017, the reward is only 12.5 Bitcoins per block and this value will decrease by half every 210,000 blocks. As more and more Bitcoins are created, the amount of computing power involved and difficulty of the mining process increases.

Because only 21million Bitcoins will ever be created, the issuance is regulated by an algorithm software which adjusts the difficulty of the Proof of Work problem frequently. Difficulty adjustment depends on how quickly blocks are solved within a certain timeframe and is approximately every two weeks or 2016 blocks. It takes, on average, about ten minutes to process a block. Mining is designed in the way that the block reward in the form of new Bitcoins (new Bitcoins issued) is halved every four years. The next halving is expected to happen at the end of May 2020. After that the mining rewards will drop from 12.5 Bitcoins per block, to 6.25 Bitcoins per block.

Why 10 minutes?

That is the amount of time that the Bitcoin developers think is necessary for a steady and diminishing flow of new coins until the maximum number of 21 million is reached (expected sometime in 2140).

Bitcoin mining offers many functions to blockchain technology. However, the most important functions are:

Issuance of new Bitcoins: When miners verify a transaction and solve the hard equation of blockchain with their specialized computers, they are rewarded with a certain unit of Bitcoin. The number of Bitcoins rewarded to miners depends on the computing power that they contribute to generate new Bitcoins.

Confirming transactions: When a transaction shows on the blockchain, before I can be completed between two parties involved, miners must validate it. When the transaction is confirmed, then both parties rewarded equally. Once a transaction is included in the block, it is officially embedded into Bitcoin's blockchain.

Security: Miners secure the Bitcoin network by making it difficult to attack or adjust. So the more miners that mine Bitcoin, the more the network gets secure. Why? Because the only way a Bitcoin transaction can be reversed is to have more than 51% of the hash power. The distributed hash power among different miners keeps the network safe and more secure.

Bitcoin mining is very similar to the mining of other commodities. It takes time and processes at a slow rate. In the past, people could make substantial profits from mining using just an ordinary desktop computer or laptop. Now for Bitcoin mining to be profitable, miners must use industrial-grade mining hardware like Application Specific Integrated Circuits (ASIC), more advanced processing units like Graphic Processing Units (GPUs) and cheap electricity because it requires high consumption.

Chapter Six

Understanding altcoins

The governments of the world have spent hundreds and hundreds of trillions of dollars bailing out a decaying, Dickensian, outmoded system called banking, when the solution to the future of finance is peer-to-peer. It's going to be alternative currencies like Bitcoin and it's not actually going to be a banking system as we had before 2008.

What is altcoin?

Among all the cryptocurrencies Bitcoin is the most recognizable and dominant digital currency with around 67% of market capitalization share in the crypto market. Bitcoin is the most well-known cryptocurrency as it is the first decentralized digital currency. Today Bitcoin is considered to be "a gold of the Internet" as it introduced blockchain technology to the entire world. Most currencies are issued by a central authority, which controls the money supply. Bitcoin's main purpose was to decentralize currencies so that the government isn't in control of our money. Bitcoin is independent from world governments, banks, financial institutions and corporations.

Bitcoin is the money of the people as no authority can interfere in Bitcoin transactions, impose transactions fees or take money away; fiat currency is the money of the government. Over time, the adoption of Bitcoin and blockchain technology has triggered the launch of many other digital currencies collectively referred to as altcoins.

The word 'altcoin' is an abbreviation for 'Bitcoin alternative' and thus is a common name for any single digital cryptocurrency similar to Bitcoin. Altcoins are referred to as Bitcoin alternatives because they hope to either replace or improve upon at least one Bitcoin component.

Since they were inspired by Bitcoin, they have tried to present themselves as modified versions of Bitcoin. Therefore, many of these altcoins are a result of 'forks' of Bitcoin built on its own source code. As they are built on various algorithms, altcoins have different properties and characteristics.

While some of these currencies are easier to mine than Bitcoins, there are trade-offs, including greater risk brought by lesser liquidity, acceptance and value retention. Altcoins may differ from Bitcoin in every possible way, such as the degree of decentralization, mining structure, coin supply methods, less volatile, transactions speed, privacy and so on.

Some of these cryptocurrencies outperform Bitcoin by offering a higher number of transactions or lower transaction fees. Many analysts believe that in the future, a few cryptocurrencies might become more valuable than the 'father of coins' Bitcoin.

All alternative cryptocurrencies are mathematically-based, incredibly transparent and driven by blockchain-based software. They can be classified into the following groups:

Decentralized digital cryptocurrencies

- These are virtual, based on blockchain technology, cryptocurrencies which are used for the sole purpose of making or receiving secure online payments. They are not issued or controlled by any central authority. For instance, the most popular cryptocurrencies are Litecoin, Monero, ZCash, Dash. These cryptocurrencies have their own dedicated blockchain and are primarily used as a medium for digital payments.

Crypto tokens

- Crypto tokens are a special kind of virtual currency tokens that represent a particular asset or a utility on a blockchain. They often operate on top of the blockchain that is created using the standard templates like Ethereum, EOS, NEO, Cardano. Such a blockchain acts as a medium for creation and execution of smart contracts or decentralized applications (Dapps), where the programmable, self-executing code is used to process and manage the various transactions. And the crypto tokens are used to facilitate these transactions. For example, a crypto token that gives entitlement to the token holder to view 24 hours of streaming content on a video-sharing blockchain.

Stable coins

- Stable coins have become the fastest growing category in the blockchain ecosystem. Stable coins are a new type of cryptocurrency that are designed to minimize the effects of price volatility and meant to hold stable values. This cryptocurrency is pegged to another real-world stable asset like gold or the US dollar. As a result, its value should remain relatively stable over the longer time period.

Sometimes price volatility makes cryptocurrencies unsuitable for everyday payments. Hence, stable coins could provide a price-stable solution and function as a medium of monetary exchange. For example, Tether, USD Coin, TrueUSD, Gemini Dollar are 'stable coins' cryptocurrencies. Stable coins are not as exciting as speculative assets, mainly because their backers supply only the portion that they can back against a stable real-world asset. They are highly attractive tools when it comes to retaining the qualities of blockchain-enabled payment networks for, say, remittance and hedging.

State-owned cryptocurrency

-        This is also a new class of blockchain-based cryptocurrencies that are issued by central banks and act as national digital currencies. These cryptocurrencies are designed to be used as a medium of exchange inside the country and regulated by the governments. A state-owned digital currency would normally have to be backed by a national fiat currency at rate 1:1 or backed by a country's commodity reserves. Venezuela has led the way with the Petro crypto coin backed by oil, and now Cambodia, Iran, Russia, Turkey, Sweden, Ukraine, and many other nations are considering introducing their own state-backed cryptocurrencies.

The city of Calgary has announced its intention to launch its own cryptocurrency. The currency is to be known as 'Calgary Digital Dollar'. And it will be used only within the Calgary city in the Alberta Province in Canada.

Choosing the best altcoin could be a difficult task due to many options available on the market. Moreover, you have to consider and prioritize which main characteristics you are going to go for. Later in this book, I will cover the most promising eight coins which have great future potential.

The easiest way to buy altcoins is through online crypto exchanges such as Coinbase, Kraken, Poloniex, Bitfinex. Bittrex, Binance or KuCoin. You can choose any other well-established cryptocurrency exchange depending on your geographical location. Some of these places (Coinbase, Kraken) offer you a small variety of coins which you can acquire with a credit card or traditional money (fiat currency) via bank transfer. Many other crypto exchanges (Binance, Bittrex, etc) have the largest selection of altcoins which can be bought only with Bitcoin and Ethereum. So if you are planning to add more coins to your portfolio, then you will have to buy Bitcoin or Ethereum first and send them to these exchanges.

Initial Coin Offering (ICO) could be another excellent investment opportunity for early investors. It has always been a good strategy to include a few recently launched new digital cryptocurrencies in your portfolio. During ICO, new crypto coins are released at a discounted price before they get listed on exchanges. And once the cryptocurrency project succeeds in the future, it can provide you with a substantial return on your investment.

Chapter Seven

Initial Coin Offering

Legitimate ICOs & 'Altcoin' have become way to invest in innovative blockchain projects.

What does ICO mean?

Currently there are over 4,000 altcoins and tokens created by developers that are available in the digital market. The developers introduce a new digital cryptocurrency via a crowd sales method called Initial Coin offering (ICO), which refers to the creation and sale of a certain amount of digital currency. The tokens they sell create incentives and perform basic functions in the system they are building. It is the way for many entrepreneurs to raise funds for their new digital cryptocurrency venture projects or to launch new digital services and applications. The new coins are often released at a discounted price in exchange for fiat currency or other well-established cryptocurrency such as Bitcoin or Ethereum. ICO could be an excellent investment opportunity for early investors if the project goals are accomplished and the cryptocurrency succeeds and appreciates in value.

Nowadays, this is a 'digital way' of raising funds for future development of the company and is very similar to Initial Public Offering (IPO), where traditional companies go public and earn funds from individual investors by selling their shares. The ICO projects sell virtual coins often referred to as cryptocurrency tokens, which are similar to shares.

In the 'digital era', tech companies prefer to raise funds via ICO for a number of reasons:

- Having full control of a business and not sharing it with investors, like with shares.
- With ICO funds can be raised globally from anywhere in the world.
- ICOs are largely unregulated. It means that no bureaucracy is involved which could take up to a few months for the start-up company to access the market. Moreover, there are no government organizations overseeing ICOs.
- ICOs are decentralized meaning that no single central authority is governing them.

Companies are looking for financial support from early investors who are interested in the offerings and buy new cryptocurrency tokens specific to the ICO. The companies use the investors' money to fund their projects, while investors contribute their money and hope that the tokens will perform well in the future and provide them with a high return on their investments.

A new study was carried out by the Boston College during which 4,003 ICOs were examined. The investigation found that investors earn on average a return of 82% within 60 days of a token release, after 3 months the average return is 140%, after 6 months 430%. However, every investment should first be thoroughly researched before a decision is made. There are many fraudulent ICOs which offer fake 'white paper' and potential buyers are often caught by counterfeit ICOs. Moreover, a large number of cryptocurrencies that have performed an ICO lose their value or simply disappear after some time. Finally, it puts an investment at risk due to no protection from unregulated financial activities. Therefore, investing in ICOs can be a real means to gain substantial profits within a short period of time and at the same time, very risky.

It doesn't matter if you are new in the crypto world looking to invest in something or an expert. All you need is an informational step-by-step guide that will help you understand how to invest in real ICOs. Then if you are ready to buy an ICO, you will need cryptocurrency and a cryptocurrency wallet. Any combination of digital coins and wallet may be requested for a given ICO. However, in most cases, you specifically need Ethereum and a MyEtherWallet (or a full Ethereum wallet). This is because many ICOs are token-based systems built on the Ethereum blockchain platform.

By the way, Ethereum was one of the most successful and largest token sales in history which appeared in 2014. During its release, 50 million ethers were created and sold to the public raising over US$18 million.

Successful ICO tokens are usually listed on different cryptocurrency exchanges, where initial buyers can sell their holdings and new buyers can come at any time. Main benefits for ICO buyers are the access to the services that the token is providing and gains through a future increase in the token's price. These gains can be realized at any time by selling them on an exchange.

As the cryptocurrency market is growing, there are more new types of blockchain business start-up companies emerging, inspired by a new funding system and operating structure. At the time this book was written, the number of all digital currencies recently surpassed 3,000. In 2017, 1,069 ICO projects were launched for the entire year. And in just the first half of 2018, there have been another 2,131 projects recorded.

ICO Rating is an independent rating agency that conducts analytical research evaluating ICOs and the ICO market. According to their market report for the second quarter of 2018, ICOs in 2018 have already raised over US$11 billion in investments and outpaced the whole of 2017. Most of the funds were raised in financial services, banking and payments, and blockchain infrastructure industries. As the blockchain technology market matures, it looks like the growth in Initial Coins Offerings and quality will continue to improve. As per the ICO Rating report, Europe has recently become a leader in launching 46% of all ICO projects, while the US is leading in investment, collecting 65% of funds. It was noted that the 'most favourable' ecosystems for ICOs were created in the US, Switzerland and Singapore.

As we can see, ICOs have rapidly come to dominate attention in the cryptocurrency and blockchain industries. They have established an effective and efficient way to raise capital and could help to integrate capital markets around the world.

After you have learned about cryptocurrency and the blockchain technology, perhaps you should look into researching and buying ICOs in order to increase gains on your investments.

Chapter Eight

How to select alternative cryptocurrencies

Cryptocurrency will be everywhere and the world will have to readjust.

Choosing the right altcoin

When it comes to choosing alternative cryptocurrencies for your portfolio, you have a wide range of available coins. For someone who is experienced in the cryptocurrency world and knows about coins that have potential to increase in value, it should not be a problem. However, if you are new to this industry, you will have no idea how to make the safest choice. As beginners, we tend to go after the rapid price increase rather than considering the technical properties and characteristics of the project, real-world use cases, future development perspectives and mass adoption.

So how do you select alternative cryptocurrencies for your portfolio and secure a good return on your investment?

In order to make the right choice, you have to do thorough research on coins and consider which main characteristics you are going to go for. The best place which offers an exhaustive listing of all virtual coins and tokens is CoinMarketCap. If you intend to build a strong portfolio, then this website is a starting point for you.

CoinMarketCap contains comprehensive data about all cryptocurrencies that are ranked accordingly to their popularity and market cap value. Moreover, it provides current market price information, maximum and circulating supply, average trading daily volume and percentage change. Here you can also find the list of exchanges where you can buy a particular cryptocurrency.

In the cryptocurrency market, price trends play a major role in analyzing the behavior of the market. Hence, with CoinMarketCap you will be able to look at the historical price data and analyse the graph charts. This is a very helpful price analysis technique which will help you to understand the past performance of the digital asset and see how the coin grows over time. It will definitely help you to make better investment decisions. Thus, CoinMarketCap could be a useful tool when you start investing in cryptocurrencies.

In addition to the technical price analysis, you will also need to understand the fundamentals behind each cryptocurrency project. Therefore, you will have to go to the official website of any particular cryptocurrency that is listed on CoinMarketCap. Simply click on the name of the coin that you are interested in and then go to its website home page. There you will have access to all the information about the digital asset including the 'white paper'.

The 'white paper' is an informational document which is designed to help you to understand the purpose and development of the project better. Hence, before you choose an altcoin for your portfolio, read the white paper and learn in detail about the project:

- What the idea is behind the project and what it has to offer.
- Does the crypto project introduce an improved solution to a common real life, business, economy or technical challenge?
- Try to understand the technical features of a particular offering.
- Does the project have a clear strategic development plan and well-defined roadmap for the future?
- Look for information about developers and see if there is a robust team behind the project.

Lastly, find out if the crypto project has a vibrant community, check forums and social networks, and research on feedback about the altcoins. It is a great practice to join various Telegram and Reddit groups of the cryptocurrency that has caught your attention. By doing this, you will get to know about other people's opinions on the project. As a bonus, you might also get a chance to even interact with some of the core team members of the project. This would be very helpful when you are choosing a cryptocurrency to invest in.

There is always a risk involved when you are investing in a digital asset. In a world where many new altcoins are being launched, there could be developers who may want to take undue advantage of the newcomers into the industry. They will offer lucrative profits in the beginning, only to disappear from the market after a short while. However, it doesn't mean that every altcoin out there is a scam or part of a fraudulent scheme. Even if the ICO team is honest, the chances that their coin will become successful in the long-run might be small.

So be careful and never invest in any alternative cryptocurrencies without doing thorough research. This is why you should take your time to read the white paper of the project, research the team and check feedback on social media. Make sure that the altcoin has a purpose in the future. Even though the price of a coin is on the rise right now, a coin without a good project cannot survive on a long run. Hence, don't be tempted by just its low valuation and avoid investing a large portion of your capital in such a venture.

Of course, there are numerous projects which are ambitious in nature and have had positive ramifications. But we still have to be careful in choosing the good apple among the bad ones.

So in order to find the right ICO project, do your own thorough research and make sure that you are fully informed of the upcoming project. Know the risks involved and what precautions to take in order to avoid making incorrect investment decisions. And hopefully you will be rewarded with high returns!

Chapter Nine

Promising cryptocurrencies of the future

Cryptocurrency may hold long-term promise, particularly if the innovations promote a faster, more secure and more efficient payment system.

What digital currencies have potential?

The true potential of blockchain technology was explored only when alternative cryptocurrencies such as Ethereum came into existence. This changed the dynamic of the entire crypto market. New altcoins have been created and introduced to the cryptocurrency market which expanded at a rapid pace.

Today, with over 4,000 cryptocurrencies in existence, the price per coin ranges from a few cents to even a few hundred dollars. Even though they are built along the basic principles of Bitcoin, altcoins seek to improve a wide variety of areas and are aimed towards various goals. Consequently, based on the performance, digital currencies do not follow the same price trend and have different opportunities for an increase in value. Thus, over the past couple of years the value of some altcoins has increased by hundreds percentages and even outperformed Bitcoin.

This is why building a diversified portfolio is extremely helpful when investing in cryptocurrencies. Having different digital assets in your basket can be extremely rewarding, especially when the value of some cheaper altcoins goes extremely high. In this chapter, I will discuss the most promising cryptocurrencies that could have the maximum potential for success in the crypto industry.

So what are the most popular cryptocurrencies?

Bitcoin, Ethereum, Litecoin, Ripple, EOS, Tron, Stellar, and IOTA belong to the group of most promising projects in the crypto markets. Let's take a look at these digital currencies that, over time, will have a great chance to be widely used for regular day-to day transactions.

Bitcoin (BTC) is the original decentralized cryptocurrency that was introduced to the world in 2009. It is the most recognizable and widely used cryptocurrency to date that started it all. Bitcoin is often called the 'father of coins', as it triggered the launch of other virtual currencies and continues to lead them in terms of market capitalization, user base and popularity. Nowadays, Bitcoin dominates on the crypto market with a share of approximately 67% in total. Its good reputation and large user base make this digital currency the most valuable. This is the currency that outperformed gold and is generating more annual gains over the last five years. Bitcoin is still an experimental new currency but is entering the mainstream fast and has the potential to become a universal store of value.

Ethereum (ETH) is the second best digital currency of the crypto space. Vitalik Buterin is the creator of Ethereum. He first discovered blockchain and cryptocurrency technologies in 2011 and was excited by their potential. After two and a half years he wrote the Ethereum white paper in November 2013. Launched in 2015, Ethereum was designed to be a decentralized software platform that runs smart contracts and used for enterprise solutions.

Developers use this programmable currency for building different distributed apps and technologies that wouldn't work with Bitcoin. Applications run on a custom blockchain and cryptographic ether token. They are exactly as they were programmed without possibility of downtime, censorship, fraud or third party involvement. This enables developers to create markets, tradeable digital tokens that can be used as a currency, a representation of an asset, move funds in accordance with instructions and many other things all without a middleman or counterparty risk.

In 2016 Ethereum was split into two different cryptocurrencies – Ethereum (ETH) and Ethereum Classic (ETC). There are many great projects and digital tokens already being built on Ethereum. Bloomberg has described Ethereum as the hottest new platform in the world of cryptocurrencies and Bitcoin's top rival which has future potential.

Litecoin (LTC) is another peer-to-peer global decentralized cryptocurrency based on blockchain technology and is highly ranked among the top ten altcoins. An open-source project that was created by former Google engineer Charlie Lee and launched in the year 2011, Litecoin is one of the oldest altcoins which was created with the intention to become the 'digital silver' compared to Bitcoin's 'digital gold'.

Litecoin is a global payment network that is not controlled by a third party and uses 'script' as a proof of work. It is a fork of Bitcoin and has almost the same properties as its predecessor. However, it has a faster block generation rate and hence can confirm near-zero cost transactions four times faster. Moreover, it features improved storage efficiency compared to the leading currency Bitcoin.

Litecoin can be used to purchase services such as website development or to buy goods like flights or food. They are accepted by more retailers than other cryptocurrencies. This digital currency provides a safe and easy way for merchants to accept money as there are no fees to receive money. Due to substantial industry support, trade volume and liquidity, the popularity of Litecoin is growing among developers and merchants every day. It is a proven medium of commerce with Litecoin transactions now even available via encrypted messenger app Telegram.

Ripple (XRP) is, unlike most cryptocurrencies, a centralized payment network that doesn't use blockchain technology. It is an open-source protocol that enables banks to settle international low-cost transactions worldwide in real time with peer-to-peer transparency. The first thing to know is that Ripple is both a platform and currency.

The Ripple platform is designed to allow fast and cheap transaction settlements. XRP consistently handles up to 1,500 transactions per second with each payment settled in 4 seconds on average. The platform has its own currency (XRP), which is used for representing the transfer of value across the Ripple Network. It also allows everybody to use the platform to create their own via RippleNet.

RippleNet is a network of institutional payment providers such as banks and money service businesses that use solutions developed by Ripple. Ripple's consensus ledger is a method of confirmation transactions that doesn't require mining and reduces the usage of computing power. All the tokens are initially mined and already exist. This feature makes Ripple different from other digital currencies.

Virtual currency Ripple is being used more for institutional (banks, digital assets exchanges, payment providers) or enterprise solutions around the world. It is becoming more popular with payment providers using XRP to expand reach into new markets. By using the Ripple protocol, banks can initiate money transfers across borders and have it verified within a few minutes. This would normally take several days, if not weeks, if we continued to use traditional transfer methods.

By partnering with several centralized institutes, Ripple has secured its spot as a major player in the financial industry. It is being supported by Santander, American Express, Credit Union, MoneyGram, Westpac, BBVA, UBS and many others. Although it isn't a popular cryptocurrency in the crypto world, no one can deny the success Ripple has had over the past few years.

EOS (EOS) is a relatively new altcoin that had the most successful crowd sales in 2018 and raised US$2.5 billion. The Ethereum network revolutionized blockchain technology, by widening its use cases. However, it still had some major issues. Some of the most pressing issues were the slow transaction speed and the high transaction fee that one had to cough up. Thus, EOS came into existence.

EOS provides a platform for developers to build decentralized applications. Unlike Ethereum, where users had to pay a fee each time they executed a smart contract, on the EOS network the users buy a portion of the network whenever they buy the EOS tokens. The computational power of the portion that you own would then be used for executing any smart contracts on the network.

The scalability of the EOS network is the main reason for its success. The features provided by the EOS network, along with its scalability will play a major role in the development of blockchain. The EOS project has had some major developments over the recent past. EOS even converted from their token platform to their own blockchain. Numerous hackathons promoting the development on the EOS platform were also organized. Additionally, around US$200 million was invested by a VC partner for the development of EOS in the Asian region.

EOS makes it easy for companies to use its platform in order to create and run multiple decentralized apps. This significantly reduces the IT infrastructure need of the company and makes it more attractive for enterprise clients. As more and more companies start using the EOS blockchain-based platform for their decentralized applications, the valuation of this platform will increase.

Tron (TRX) was one of the most controversial altcoins of 2017. However, since then, it has found its way back. Tron combines the solution provided by the Ethereum network, with a supercharged version of the blockchain. The Tron network is extremely fast and cheap at processing transactions. The main mission of Tron is to leverage blockchain technology in the entertainment sector. Thus far, the various acquisitions made by Tron are helping it move towards achieving this goal.

Tron is one of the few cryptocurrencies that went through hell and made it back. Initially, Tron gained a lot of support from people around the world.

However, this support was short-lived. Soon, prices of Tron plummeted; however, these prices soon stabilized. This was due to the revamped project and various partnerships.

Tron partnered with Baidu, which is one of the most reputed search engines in China. While Baidu benefits from the blockchain technology of Tron, Tron benefits from the cloud technology provided by Baidu. Tron also acquired BitTorrent, which is a popular media sharing technology. As Tron mainly focuses on the development of media, working alongside BitTorrent is going to help out a lot.

The Tron blockchain now has over 1 million user accounts and has reached over 100 million recorded contracts. The number of TRON addresses, or users, is growing by between 10,000 and 40,000 per day. All these reasons mean Tron remains one of the top
cryptocurrencies in the world.

Stellar (XLM) is considered by many in the crypto world to be the better counterpart of the Ripple project. Not only is Stellar a fork of the Ripple code but was also created by a co-founder of Ripple. Similar to Ripple, Stellar also aims at providing a solution to centralized financial transactions for individuals. One of the goals of the Stellar project is to account for 60% of all cross-border peer-to-peer transactions in the future. The Stellar network uses a new consensus mechanism that makes transaction verification extremely fast while not compromising on security. It provides the perfect solution for cross-border transactions, as these payments can be sent without any fee.

Hence, whilst Ripple creates applications for banks, Stellar creates applications for regular people, particularly the 'unbanked'. Stellar is also more typically 'blockchain' in its organization, plans and user base. Furthermore, developers create DApps on Stellar to be used in public blockchain/tech markets Thus, Stellar has a major role to play in the future of the finance industry.

Stellar is the decentralized variation of Ripple's codebase. It is one of the few coins that managed to secure the spot as one of the top fifteen cryptocurrencies, even during the bear market phase. Stellar has introduced a fast and low-fee decentralized exchange (DEX), putting it far ahead of most crypto exchanges.

Another main reason for its popularity is partnerships with various centralized corporations. Stellar has partnered with IBM, helping them in the development of their own blockchain. Several banks also use the Stellar network to process near real-time cross-border transactions. Some of the other notable partnerships of Stellar include Deloitte, Stripe and the Pioneer app.

IOTA (MIOTA) – the decentralized crypto world offers a lot of solutions to several current day problems. The same goes for the Internet of Things (IoT) technology. The marvels that these two can achieve when combined together, is truly amazing. And IOTA does just that. IOTA provides a blockless blockchain, which helps all the IoT sensors to stay connected and synchronized with each other. The data of one sensor is always available to all the sensors connected through IOTA.

Additionally, all transactions on the IOTA network are free of cost, extremely fast and highly secure. This provides the ideal conditions required by the IoT sensors to perform efficiently.

The IOTA project has seen some major developments during its existence. To start things off, the IOTA network uses Directed Acyclic Graphs (DAG) over a traditional blockchain to record all transactions. This is the reason for its fast and cheap transactions. IOTA has also recently partnered with Microsoft.

The software giant has a separate branch dedicated to IoT devices and by partnering with IOTA, it aims to create smarter cities worldwide. Some of the other IOTA partnerships include Bosch. Together, they aim at connecting over 15.6 billion devices by the year 2020. IOTA is also partnered with several other organizations including Volkswagen, Fujitsu, Orange, etc. We are not very far away from living in a world in which all devices are connected to a single network.

The promising cryptocurrencies mentioned in this chapter have shown great development stability and even survived during the 2018 bear market. Thus, having them in your portfolio is a great way to add extra diversity while also leaving it open for growth opportunity. However, ensure that you do your own research before you invest in any cryptocurrency.

Chapter Ten

History of Bitcoin and who is Satoshi Nakamoto?

We have elected to put our money and faith in a mathematical framework that is free of politics and human error.

The motivation behind Bitcoin creation

The libertarians believed that freedom was the right that was stolen from every one of us. As long as the centralized monetary system existed, no one could enjoy complete financial freedom.

All our financial transactions are being constantly monitored. Moreover, there is very little transparency of the money that we keep in banks. The centralized banks control and use our money for their own benefits, and we do not receive anything in return. It is not surprising that financial privacy and freedom are taken away from us in such a centralized society that has existed for many years.

Why was Bitcoin created?

Many people believe that The Bretton Woods Agreement and The Global Recession created the permanent shortcomings which surrounded the existing monetary and banking system. Moreover, these financial events brought out the problems associated with having to store our money with centralized banks and financial institutions. People lost their trust in banks and started to wish for a new system, demanding full control of their own money. Perhaps, they realized the need for a currency that would not be controlled by any central authority.

If you want to understand more about the origin of Bitcoin, perhaps it may be useful to know about these economic downturns.

The Bretton Woods Agreement

Back in July 1944, delegates from 44 different countries met during a monetary and financial conference held in Bretton Woods, New Hampshire to discuss and agree on a new international monetary system. Under the Bretton Woods Agreement, currencies were linked to the price of gold, and the US dollar was established as a global reserve currency, linked to the price of gold. The agreement set fixed foreign exchange rates and made currencies convertible to the dollar. Hence, countries settled their international balances in dollars, while US dollars were fully convertible to gold at the price of US$35 per ounce.

Keeping the price of gold at a fixed rate and adjusting the supply of dollars was the responsibility of the United States. However, as the demand for dollars kept increasing, the US government was printing more notes which exceeded the amount of gold in its reserve.

In 1971, the Bretton Wood system eventually failed when many foreign countries demanded gold in exchange for dollars they received through international trade. As a result, the US gold reserve (and the world's largest) diminished rapidly and there just wasn't enough gold to back the US dollars supplied.

On 15 August 1971, the US President Richard Nixon, terminated convertibility of dollar to gold (Gold Standard) for the central banks of other countries and brought the Bretton Woods system to an end. Therefore, the US dollar failed to secure its spot as a global currency.

Since that time there hasn't been any real attempt at creating another global currency. Only at the beginning of 1988 the proposal to create a universal world currency in the form of Phoenix appeared. However, mankind was not prepared for such a great leap at that time and the idea of the Phoenix global currency faded into oblivion.

The Great Recession of 2008

With the financial markets controlled by only a few major players, there was a very high imbalance of power. We were all led to believe that we were in full control of our money. However, that wasn't the case. During the 2008 Global Financial Crisis, there was a hype created across several investment plans, some being loans riskier than the others. The money that people had saved up in their accounts was used by banks and invested in some high-risk mortgage related schemes only to pursue larger profits.

However, this backfired after the dangerous 'investment bubble' burst. Several bonds that many financial institutions invested in were worth nothing. As this phenomenon occurred all around the world, it resulted in the global financial meltdown.

The unemployment rate rose dramatically and nearly 9 million people around the world lost their jobs. Perhaps all this was nothing when compared to the crisis in countries such as Greece, Cyprus, Zimbabwe, etc. The global financial crisis combined with the economic mismanagement of these countries led to a massive inflation of their local currency and made it practically worthless.

We have experienced the worst recession since the Great Depression in the 1930s. Both financial downturns were linked around centralized fiat currency. Thus, the need for a decentralized universal currency that is not being controlled by government authorities emerged. This was the main motivation behind the creation of the first decentralized cryptocurrency Bitcoin.

On the 31st of October 2008, the world saw the release of the Bitcoin white paper, or as it was known, *Bitcoin: A Peer-to-Peer Electronic Cash System.* The white paper was published on metzdowd.com's cryptography mailing list and described Bitcoin as a currency that solves the problem of double spending, so as to prevent the currency from being copied. Offering a decentralized peer-to-peer digital payment network, cryptocurrency Bitcoin proposed a system that replaces the need for central authorities like banks and financial institutions.

On the 3rd of January 2009, the genesis block of Bitcoin was mined and it rewarded the miner with 50 Bitcoins (including the text 'The Times 03/Jan/ 2009 Chancellor on brink of second bailout for banks'). January 9th, 2009 is remembered as the day when an open-source version 1.0 of Bitcoin software code was released. It included a Bitcoin generation system that would create a total of 21 million Bitcoins through to the year 2140.

For the initial few days, we could only see the new blocks that were created and mined. The very first transaction of Bitcoin currency was made on the 12th of January 2009 after block 170 was mined. It took place between Satoshi and a cryptographic developer named Hal Finney. This is when the true power of cryptocurrency was realized.

Who is Satoshi Nakamoto?

Everyone knows that Bitcoin was developed by a single person or group of people under the name of Satoshi Nakamoto. However, the true identity of Satoshi remains unknown. With Satoshi not coming out of hiding, people are left to only speculate as to who this anonymous creator is.

On a P2P Foundation profile, Satoshi Nakamoto claimed to be a 37-year-old programmer living in Japan. However, because of his perfect English and his software not being labelled in Japanese, there are some doubts about this.

Over a period of several years there have been rumors about the real identity of the Bitcoin creator. The mass media believed that behind the name Satoshi Nakamoto were a professor of economics and law Nick Sabo, the owner of anonymous trading platform 'Silk Road' Ross Ulbricht, and Japanese mathematician Motidzuki Siniti. However, all of them publicly denied being behind the Satoshi pseudonym.

Then in March 2014, Newsweek published an article claiming that a computer engineer living in Temple City in Los Angeles County was the creator of Bitcoin. However, 64-year-old Dorian Prentis Satoshi Nakamoto, an American of Japanese origin, made a denial in the mass media that he was the shadowy force behind Bitcoin.

In early 2018, searches revealed that American computer scientist Dave Kleiman could have been one of the figures behind the Satoshi Nakamoto identity. Although there is a little information about Kleiman on the Internet, it's been suggested that he created Bitcoin. Surprisingly, he has links to Craig Wright during the early days of Bitcoin development. Craig Wright is an Australian computer scientist who has publicly claimed to be Satoshi Nakamoto.

It's unclear if Dave Kleiman and Craig Wright actually created Bitcoin, but there is no doubt that both men were business partners in the past. They were two of the first people involved with Bitcoin, mining Bitcoin and sending Bitcoin transactions. From their collaboration in 2008 until 2013, Wright and Kleiman were able to mine over a million Bitcoins. On January 12, 2009, Wright, Kleiman and two others sent each other Bitcoin transactions recorded on the blockchain. These were some of the first transactions on the Bitcoin network.

Wright and Kleiman allegedly entered a contract securing Bitcoins between the two. Neither could access the Bitcoins without the others permission. Dave Kleiman's death could be the reason why Satoshi's Bitcoins have not been moved yet. They are unable to be moved until the trust releases them, something that is scheduled to take place in 2020. Those Bitcoins are now disputed between Wright and Kleiman's estate. Self-proclaimed Satoshi

Craig Wright is being sued by Kleiman's family on accusations that he defrauded and stole over US$11 billion worth of Bitcoins and hard drives from Dave Kleiman.

Craig Wright, who has identified himself as Satoshi Nakamoto, also claims that he had partnered with Dave to create and mine Bitcoin. The two met in an online cryptography forum in 2003 and were connected by a long time interest in cybersecurity and digital forensics. Craig appears to downplay Kleiman's role in the development of Bitcoin, claiming he just created the whitepaper while Craig did most of the coding. Emails show that Wright contacted Kleiman in the months leading up to the release of the Bitcoin whitepaper. Some claim the email is fabricated – part of an elaborate joke by Craig Wright to claim he is Satoshi. Others claim it shows definitive proof that Craig Wright and Dave Kleiman created Bitcoin.

Without a doubt, Dave Kleiman and Craig Wright were both around during the early days of Bitcoin. It's certainly possible that both played the role of Satoshi Nakamoto. It's also possible that neither developed Bitcoin, and that they were just prominent miners and crypto enthusiasts. Ultimately, the mystery of Dave Kleiman is one of the biggest mysteries surrounding the Bitcoin community.

The most recent Satoshi candidate is Paul Solotshi Calder Le Roux, a 46-year-old genius programmer and creator of an open-source encryption software E4M and TrueCrypt, and author of a publication with similar spelling and language in his writing style to the one in Bitcoin's whitepaper. He also had an extensive criminal background and was involved in drug and arms trafficking, gold smuggling, precious metals mining, money laundering, assassinations and more. The brilliant software developer has been in jail since 2012. Perhaps, this is the reason why his one million Bitcoins haven't been touched.

Evidence suggests that the criminal mastermind Paul Le Roux is Satoshi. He was familiar with the C++ programming language and had an obsession with cryptography and privacy, much like Satoshi Nakamoto. Satoshi's one million Bitcoins are allegedly locked away in secure disk encryption software TrueCrypt developed by Le Roux.

Both Satoshi Nakamoto and Paul Le Roux were concerned about the centralized power of authority and expressed this in a similar way in their E4M manifesto and Bitcoin whitepaper. They understood that a new digital payment method was needed to improve the difficulties of traditional payment systems. Paul Le Roux had participated in online gambling activities, and Bitcoin's initial code had a poker 'client' included.

Satoshi disappeared in early 2011 to 'move on to other things'. Around the same time, Le Roux transitioned from his field of software development to cartel boss. Despite all of the evidence that suggests Le Roux could be Satoshi Nakamoto, the true identity of the Bitcoin creator hasn't been confirmed and still remains a mystery.

Lately, there have also been some other claims by people who call themselves Satoshi Nakamoto. But none have been able to successfully produce the evidence required to support their claims.

Some believe that Bitcoin was actually developed by an Artificial Intelligence. There have also been many conspiracy theories that even link the CIA (Central Intelligence Agency) to Bitcoin creation. But the wildest theory among all of them has to be that Bitcoin was developed by four Asian companies: Samsung, Toshiba, Nakamichi, and Motorola.

Satoshi Nakamoto has never revealed his true identity to anyone and participated with others involved in the project via mailing lists. He used an email address from an anonymous mail hosting service for all his communications with a team of crypto developers working on the further improvement of open-source code. Then he finally began to fade from the community towards the end of 2010. The last known communication from Satoshi was in the spring of 2011 when he said that he had 'moved on to other things'. No one has been able to communicate with him since.

Everyone is eager to know the true identity of Satoshi because of the high degree of control he has over the price of Bitcoin. The wallet address that belongs to the creator, Satoshi, is said to hold around a million Bitcoins in it. This is currently worth over US$10 billion. If Satoshi starts selling his share of Bitcoins, then the market will collapse. This is presumably the reason why Satoshi has chosen to remain anonymous.

Until now the identity of the Bitcoin founder remains a mystery. All we have is the pseudonym Satoshi Nakamoto. His accounts are no longer active and coins in his wallet have never been spent. Satoshi Nakamoto has disappeared from the world, or so it would seem.

History of Bitcoin

Bitcoin came into existence mainly to return financial freedom back to people. The centralized organizations had already abused their powers, which had resulted in multiple financial disasters in the past. The financial crisis of 2008 was the ultimate trigger that resulted in the creation of Bitcoin. While the Bitcoin white paper was published only in October of 2008, the idea for the decentralized cryptocurrency goes further back to 2007.

It is known that American computer scientist and cryptographer Nick Sabo was deeply involved in the Bitcoin project. In fact, he had discussed the idea for a decentralized cryptocurrency well before the Bitcoin white paper was even released. In 1998, Sabo designed a mechanism for a decentralized digital currency which he called 'Bit Gold'. Bit Gold was never implemented but provided a solid core foundation for the Bitcoin architecture.

According to history, Satoshi Nakamoto liked Sabo's technical description of decentralized digital currency and began working on the Bitcoin concept in 2007. Furthermore, Wei Dai's 'B-money', Adam Back's 'Hashcash' and Dr. Ralph Merkle's work on cryptographic hashing had inspired Satoshi to create the Bitcoin protocol.

After the initial idea of Bitcoin was conceived in 2007, it is believed that Satoshi Nakamoto had done tremendous research in order to create a real version of digital currency. One of the main obstacles in the way of the developers was to develop a method to avoid double spends. This would not be possible without having a centralized authentication method. This is where the revolutionary blockchain technology came into use.

There were several attempts to create decentralized currency in the past. However, all of them failed when it came to the complication of double spends. In the double spend process, users would be able to spend the same coin on multiple occasions. This would result in an individual having an unlimited supply of money.

The only method to avoid double spends was to use the centralized method wherein each and every transaction was to be confirmed by a centralized authority. This would go completely against the idea of decentralization. Thus, blockchain technology was considered to be operational.

On the Bitcoin network, each and every transaction is recorded on a public ledger called the blockchain. This is an immutable ledger and no changes can be made to it once a transaction is confirmed. In order for a transaction to be confirmed, a complex mathematical equation needs to be solved. After a particular transaction is recorded on the blockchain, the Bitcoin that was used during the transaction cannot be used by the sender again. Thus, it eliminates any chance of double spending without having to rely on any centralized methods.

All this information was included in a more concise manner and published in the form of a whitepaper on the cryptographic mailing list. This idea soon gained the attention of many people who wanted to taste financial freedom and free the world from the unhealthy practices of centralized financial organizations.

Looking at the growing support of people towards Bitcoin, it was evident that this idea could amount to something substantial. Hence, the open-source code for Bitcoin protocol was released in January of 2009. For the first few days no one knew how to use this new technology. Bitcoin was still in its initial testing phase and only on January 12th, 2009, the very first Bitcoin transaction was made between Satoshi Nakamoto and computer scientist Hal Finney.

This first Bitcoin transaction made a huge impact on the future of Bitcoin. Initially, only computer geeks would go on to download the Bitcoin client, mine their own Bitcoins and make digital crypto transactions. At that time Bitcoin did not have any true value. Then later a couple of students did an evaluation and put the price of 1 Bitcoin equal to 3 cents. For the better part, it was never about the value. People were just amused by the way the whole network functioned.

Until 2010, Bitcoin was just another virtual currency that was used by developers and computer geeks. This, however, changed when a developer named Laszlo Hanyecz bought two pizzas in exchange for 10,000 Bitcoins. This day is of great importance in the history of Bitcoin, as it was the first time that Bitcoin was used to buy something with value in the real world.

The world's most powerful central banker saved Bitcoin

After Bitcoin reached some monetary value, crypto enthusiasts decided to experiment with it. From that moment they began to use Bitcoin for purchases of goods and services online. The number of daily transactions started to grow, causing the Bitcoin network to evolve into a peer-to-peer payment system.

Unfortunately, the cryptocurrency that provides a certain degree of anonymity encouraged some of its users to utilize Bitcoin as a digital currency for dealing with drugs and money laundering.

In February 2011, American Ross Ulbricht combined two anonymous computer networks, Bitcoin and Tor, and launched the Silk Road website. Silk Road, the first online 'black market', was known as the decentralized platform for selling illegal drugs and illicit services on the Dark Web. The website was envisioned to be a 'free-market economic experiment' that was focused on user anonymity. An amateur programmer with strong libertarian and anarchist ideals, Ross Ulbricht wanted to create the marketplace that would function without government oversight. His intention was to give people the freedom to make their own choices. Ulbricht criticized government regulations and believed that 'people should have the right to buy and sell whatever they wanted so long as they weren't hurting anyone else'.

Operated under the pseudonymous 'Dread Pirate Roberts', the Silk Road platform was a safe haven alternative to the often deadly violence so common with the global drug war and unsafe street drug transactions.

While the users of the Dark Web site could use the Tor network to hide their identities, they had no way of exchanging anonymous payments among themselves. Sending envelopes full of cash via postal services was an obviously impractical solution.

Ulbricht got around this issue by testing Bitcoin as a payment method. The only identifying information needed was the Bitcoin address of the receiver. A Bitcoin address doesn't require a bank account, ID name or social security number, and is free to open and maintain. Bitcoin's decentralized ledger – the Blockchain – provided a way to verify that payments had been received or sent. The problem was solved by buyers and sellers conducting all transactions with virtual currency.

At that time, the price of a single Bitcoin had skyrocketed from around one dollar to over thirty dollars. The rise was partly attributable to the increased attention which Bitcoin received because of Silk Road.

As time went on, Bitcoin started to gain popularity as digital money for criminal activities and attract the attention of the media. While many embraced Silk Road and what it stood for, others believed that it would damage the emerging cryptocurrency Bitcoin.

Unsurprisingly, it wasn't long before an American Senator, Charles Schumer, called for the Drug Enforcement Agency and the Department of Justice to shut down Silk Road. In October 2013, the FBI arrested Ross Ulbricht in a San Francisco library while he was logged in to Silk Road as 'Dread Pirate Roberts' administrator. The site was closed down with 144,000 Bitcoins seized from Silk Road accounts.

The closure of Silk Road may have helped to remove the association between Bitcoin and crime. As the blockchain ledger provides a record of every transaction, it enabled law enforcement to track illegal transactions, despite the lack of a name or bank account attached to Bitcoin addresses. Consequently, Bitcoin was revealed to be a less than perfect currency for criminals.

The shutdown of Silk Road prompted the US Senate Committee on Homeland Security and Governmental Affairs to hold their first ever congressional hearing on virtual currencies, in particular Bitcoin. In November 2013, the hearing event entitled 'Beyond Silk Road: Potential risks, threats, and promises of virtual currencies' brought representatives from different federal agencies and the Bitcoin community to discuss the potential dangers of cryptocurrency, concerns over anonymity and lack of government regulations. Ahead of the hearing, they have been asked to provide their views about virtual currencies to the committee and submissions have been received from The Justice and Treasury Department, FBI and the US Federal Reserve.

In a letter to the committee, the Justice and Treasury Department said it recognized that Bitcoin offered 'legitimate financial services but they could be exploited by malicious actors such as drug dealers, traffickers and perpetrators of large-scale fraud schemes. The committee was told that virtual currencies have the same benefits and risks as other online payment systems.

In a letter dated September 6, 2013 and released during the hearing, US Federal Reserve Chairman Ben Bernanke called virtual currencies 'innovative payment systems' and stated that the bank had no plans to regulate virtual currency. He then described Bitcoin as perhaps holding 'long-term promise, particularly if the innovations promote a faster, more secure and more efficient payment system'.

'Although the Federal Reserve generally monitors developments in virtual currencies and other payment system innovations, it does not necessarily have authority to directly supervise or regulate these innovations or the entities that provide them to the market', Bernanke said in a letter. Mr Bernanke pointed out that 'the Federal Reserve plans to cooperate with other agencies on electronic cash and related issues such as virtual currencies. The Federal Reserve will continue to monitor developments as part of its broad interest in the safety and efficiency of the payment system'.

The Fed Chairman told the Senate Committee members that he sees far beyond the illicit uses of Bitcoin as a tool for criminals to move money around without being traced. Bernanke guarded 'welcome' to virtual currencies as an innovative new technology that will revolutionize both economics and politics. He believed that the world market trade in legitimate goods and services can work more efficiently without the 'dead hand' of the banks.

An intervention by Ben Bernanke enabled Bitcoin's enthusiasts to put the spotlight where they believe its potential value lies: as a cheaper alternative to the current system for transferring money around the world.

Many have called Bernanke's letter a 'cautious blessing' that saved Bitcoin from its disastrous ending. Sympathetic comments towards Bitcoin at the hearing sparked a new increase in the price of Bitcoin. The experimental virtual currency had risen by more than 5,000% in value that year.

The story of Silk Road undoubtedly provided significant exposure to the idea of Bitcoin and decentralized currencies. Although this left a bad impression in the minds of many who viewed Bitcoin as a tool for crime, Silk Road also provided an example of how Bitcoin could function in the real world, proving that a decentralized virtual currency was able to exist and transfer monetary value between participants in a global marketplace.

The closing down of Silk Road and hearings in front of US government committees have led many to believe that Bitcoin will gain more mainstream adoption in the future and become a global currency alternative.

Historical patterns of Bitcoin value and major price corrections

People soon began to trade Bitcoin for other valuables. This resulted in the eventual release of a dedicated Bitcoin exchange. The Bitcoin Market became the very first Bitcoin exchange which people used to buy and sell Bitcoin. Thus, the demand for Bitcoin peaked and the value of Bitcoin increased from 8 to 30 cents by the end of 2010.

As the demand for Bitcoin kept increasing, many requested WikiLeaks to accept Bitcoin as a method to tip others. However, this attempt was abruptly stopped Satoshi Nakamoto. In his email to WikiLeaks, Nakamoto expressed his concern about the cryptocurrency not being ready for such a mass adoption.

Although this initial attempt of mass-adoption was stopped, it did not stop users from continuing to use the cryptocurrency on a regular basis. As 2011 started, more Bitcoin exchanges came into existence. Additionally, more cryptocurrencies with slight variations from the original Bitcoin code came into existence. As a result of the rise in popularity around the world, the price of Bitcoin began to increase. From 2010 to 2012, there had been a steep increase in the value of Bitcoin.

Within the space of one year, the price of Bitcoin had risen to US$1 and it was becoming an interesting prospect of the future. Six months later the currency had doubled to US$2. While the Bitcoin wasn't stable at a particular price point, it has been showing the pattern of insane growth for some time. Bitcoin's first big jump happened in July 2011 when the coin exploded and the record-high US$31 was achieved. But the market soon realized that it was overvalued, and after a few months Bitcoin fell back to US$2.

A few believers of the ideals of Bitcoin held on to their coins and the market soon stabilized. A stable market attracted more people to re-evaluate their previous decision of selling Bitcoin and they started to buy it again.

December 2012 saw a healthy increase to US$13, but soon enough, the price was going to explode again. Within four months up until April 2013, the price had increased to a whopping US$266. It corrected itself later on back to US$100. Eventually, this astronomical increase in prise rose it to stardom for the very first time. Then people started debating about actual real-world scenarios with Bitcoin.

S0 2013 was the breakthrough year for the digital currency. Big companies began to favour the acceptance of Bitcoin and the blockchain publicly became a favourite subject for computer science programs. Many people then thought that Bitcoin had served its purpose and now it would settle down. But the digital currency became even more popular, with Bitcoin ATMs being set up and businesses were accepting virtual coin all around the world.

Thus, Bitcoin began its rise again and reached US$1,242 on 29 November 2013. In December 2013 the price crashed to US$600 and then rebounded to US$1,000, it crashed again to the US$500 range and eventually stabilized to the US$650–$800 range.

From past experiences, we have seen that a market that is driven by hype will never succeed. The same happened to Bitcoin. The misuse of Bitcoin on the Deep Web and other shady deals led to its downfall again. This downfall got worse when Mt. Gox, the biggest Bitcoin exchange at that time got hacked and all users of the platform lost all their money.

As a result, the price of Bitcoin took a major hit and dropped further to the US$250 mark. Many financial experts even predicted 2014 to be the end of Bitcoin. However, Bitcoin was still widely trusted by many people and from February 2014 to January 2017 the price stabilized between US$750 to US $1,000.

The year 2016 saw the rise of several cryptocurrencies with a wide array of use-cases. With the emergence of alternative cryptocurrency Ethereum, everyone was once again reminded about the usefulness of blockchain technology. Additionally, over a period of two years, the Bitcoin network had seen its own share of updates that made it even more useful. Thus, the demand for Bitcoin was on the rise again and consequently complemented its increase in value. The period between 2016 and 2017 saw Bitcoin even surpassing the value of gold.

The magical figure of US$1,000 was first breached in January 2017. The year 2017 was the wildest year by far for Bitcoin with its value increasing to US$20,000 at the end of December 2017. It is genuinely a remarkable achievement for a coin that was only worth 8 cents just eight years previously.

The prices then fell by a third in over 24 hours to merely US$13,900. February 5, 2018 was the most shocking and shook the roots of the world causing hundreds of thousands of people to lose substantial amounts of money. Bitcoin price dropped by more than 50% in 15 days falling to just

US$6,200. The hype created by Bitcoin and a few other cryptocurrencies drew the markets sky high, even questioning the value of gold at one point.

Over the ten years of its existence, Bitcoin has gone through several cycles of rapid ups and downs. Simply by looking at the past history, we can see that the price of Bitcoin has experienced five major price corrections. Every sudden increase of Bitcoin value was followed by a major drop. It is noticed that after the huge dip, Bitcoin's price retaliates with a greater force.

Five major Bitcoin 'bubbles' that are known to the world:

1.   The price of Bitcoin went from being just US$0.30 in January of 2011 to reach US$30 dollars in June of 2011. Later the price took a major hit and went as low as US$2 within the next five months. The market saw Bitcoin decrease by 93% of its maximum value.

2.   The price of Bitcoin increased from US$15 in January of 2013 to US$230 in April of the same year. While this 1,433% increase seemed really good, it plummeted down by 70% to US$68 in just 5 days after reaching the peak.

3.   From April 2013 to December 2013, the price went on to increase over 1,586% and reached its peak at US$1,147. Eventually, just like in the past, Bitcoin was not able to retain this price and went on to decrease by 85% and reached US$177 on January 14, 2015.

4. The year 2015 turned out to be very good for Bitcoin. It soon went on a rally and increased by 160% from US$177 in January 2015 to US$465 in December of the same year. This momentum was carried on to 2016 when the price increased in January 2016 to US$1,146. However, the price of Bitcoin took a hit and went down to US$775 within a few days.

5. The year 2017 was extremely prosperous to the Bitcoin world which resulted in the price of Bitcoin going from US$775 on 11 January 2017 to US$19,343 on December 16th 2017. However, 2018 was the exact opposite. The price of Bitcoin went down from US$19,343 in December 2017 to US$3,288 in December 2018, retracing itself by 83%.

Every time there is a massive increase in the value of Bitcoin, it attracts more people to use this innovative payment network. Even though the number of users and daily transactions has increased, the speed of transactions never changed and still remained the same. It is just a matter of time before the transactions scalability problem faced by Bitcoin is solved.

At this moment the Bitcoin network isn't ready for mass adoption of such magnitude. However, once the Lightning Network solution is fully implemented, we will see a rise in Bitcoin demand again. And as happened in the past, the price of Bitcoin will bounce back surpassing its previous high of US$20,000.

Chapter Eleven

Getting started with Bitcoin

'Bitcoin, and the ideas behind it, will be a disrupter to the traditional notions of currency. In the end, currency will be better for it.'

Why Bitcoin?

Initially, when the Internet first came out, people never thought they would even use it. It felt way too sophisticated and complicated for regular users. But with the help of advanced technologies the world has developed at a fast pace and in the current state of affairs almost everything is being done via the Internet.

Within the span of the last 30 years, we have moved from hand written letters to emails, mobile phones substituted land lines, instant messaging replaced texts, music, TV and photography became digital. Perhaps, with the whole world moving into the digital era, there was a need for a digital version of money to replace the outdated traditional payment network.

Hence, cryptocurrency Bitcoin was designed with the aim to exchange monetary value through the Internet. Being a digital version of our traditional money, it may look like our current payment networks such as Mastercard, Visa or PayPal. However, Bitcoin and other cryptocurrencies are more secure and advanced payment networks and have far more benefits for people. This is why Bitcoin's popularity and mainstream adoption have progressed significantly in the recent years. As a result, there are many people that use Bitcoin to pay for goods and services online in the same way as they would use debit or credit cards.

On the other hand, Bitcoin has grown tremendously in value over the time and transformed into the best performing digital asset class. In the last two years Bitcoin has gained more than 450% while stocks index S&P 500 and gold increased by 19.9% and 1.3% respectively. Thus, such a highly volatile asset has offered great investment opportunities to many long-term investors and short-term swing traders.

Therefore, there are three main reasons that should encourage you to get started with Bitcoin and cryptocurrencies:

1. You would like to understand how the Bitcoin digital payment network works and learn how to use it to make online transactions with cryptocurrencies. It is important for a new beginner to gain technical knowledge and know how to set up and secure the digital wallet, how to find places to buy and exchange Bitcoins, how to store cryptocurrency safely and make payments with it.

2. Investing in Bitcoin and cryptocurrencies generates a good rate of return. Like with any other investments, the key success is to believe in the long-term investments and to be able to hold crypto assets for at least five years. You have an intention to become the cryptocurrency investor and build your long-term portfolio.

3.   The price of Bitcoin can unpredictably increase or decrease over a short period of time. Bitcoin price volatility may offer you many potential gains. The dips and peaks should be seen as a buying or selling opportunity to make significant profits. You would like to start with Bitcoin, learn how to trade cryptocurrencies and create an additional source of income.

By now you probably have a good idea why you would like to start with Bitcoin. After reading previous chapters of this book you should be equipped with a good knowledge about Bitcoin and have a basic understanding how this blockchain-based payment network works.

About cryptocurrency wallet

Before you can use Bitcoin and other digital currencies, the first step is to download and set up a secure cryptocurrency wallet. No matter what the purpose of acquiring cryptocurrency, you're still going to need a place to store your digital assets. It is very similar to a traditional banking system. Simply, you need a bank account to store your money and make all your daily life payments. A digital cryptocurrency wallet can be considered as your 'bank account' for cryptocurrency. It is secured by cryptographic tools which help to protect your crypto funds and prevent unauthorized access to your wallet. Besides being a storage place, cryptocurrency wallets are also used for sending and receiving cryptocurrency funds. If a user transfers you a certain amount in Bitcoin, it gets reflected in your wallet. Since Bitcoin is completely decentralized, only you have complete control over it. No government authority or bank can seize your cryptocurrency or freeze your digital account.

In technical words, a cryptocurrency wallet is a software program, online service or a hardware device that stores your private and public keys and gives you access to your digital crypto assets, allowing to perform transactions with them.

The most vital thing to remember is that crypto wallets do not actually store anything. They are just a tool to read the blockchain where all your records and transactions are written. A cryptocurrency wallet interacts with and analyzes those blockchains to let you perform operations with your assets. Treat it like credentials to your email account – they don't contain anything but allow you to access your correspondence that is kept somewhere else. If you lose your credentials, you lose your assets, whatever they are.

Cryptocurrency wallets rely on your address which is similar to an account number. The Bitcoin address that you generate can stay permanently with your account. The real identification factor comes in the form of a private key. Every private key is associated with a public key which forms the basis for ensuring safer transactions.

Besides these key pairs and a Bitcoin wallet address, your Bitcoin wallet also stores a separate log of all of your incoming and outgoing transactions. Every transaction linked to your address will be stored by the Bitcoin wallet to give users an overview of their spending and receiving habits.

In order to use a cryptocurrency wallet securely you need to understand what the difference is between private and public keys. However, before the differences are explained, let's have a look at how the keys work.

Private keys are codes generated by your wallet in a cryptographic format that acts as the key to enter your account. In technical terms, a private key provides access to your account and helps verify the authenticity of your ownership. Private keys are generally a 256-bit 'hexadecimal' code which contain characters from 0–9 and A–F. A 256-bit key contains 64 characters which are generated through complex algorithms and look like this:

"2940447a4ed5eef7f46bcc185cb2f21d2a8bffcde5418156a9d1a44aa137553".

Whenever the first transaction is initiated by the user through his Bitcoin wallet, a unique private key and the associated public key are generated. Only the owner of the wallet has authority over the private key. Your private key is not disclosed to anyone except you. Once your private and public keys are generated, they are stored in your wallet. Whenever you initiate any transaction through your wallet, the private key acts as a proof of your ownership and helps to authorize your transactions.

Every transaction on the blockchain network undergoes a series of verifications once it is initiated. Any transaction that you undertake passes through the distributed nodes. Distributed nodes mean people across the blockchain network who can authorize your transactions. All transactions are digitally signed using your private key before they are broadcast on the blockchain network. The signature acts as an identifier for determining the owner of a digital wallet. Since no information about your private key is made public, it is solely your property.

Every private key has a public key associated with it. It helps in identifying whether the digital signature arose from the private key. The public key is made available to every user on the distributed nodes. One more peculiarity about the public key is that it is stored in the form of your public address which is nothing but the compressed and shortened version of your public key. Once the transaction is verified on the network, the recipient receives the desired amount.

A private key is simply an extremely large and highly random string of numbers and letters. The public key is mathematically derived from the private key. A public key can be shared with other people on the network. Public keys are used by other users on the network to challenge ownership of Bitcoins. The only way your public key, and therefore your Bitcoin, can be comprised is by revealing your private key. Hence your private key should always be kept secret. Private and public keys are one of the greatest features of cryptocurrency transactions. Unless a user is unwary of his actions, it is almost impossible to lose money.

If you want to understand the basic difference between private and public keys, let me compare it with traditional banking. Every time you wish to add an amount to your account or want someone to transfer funds to your account, you share your account number.

However, when you need to withdraw an amount from the ATM or perform an online transaction, your authentication generally takes places through a PIN or OTP. Your PIN is confidential, and it merely helps the system understand that it is indeed you who is performing the transaction.

Let me now draw the similarities between traditional banking and cryptocurrency transactions. The account number provides information about who the owner is while your PIN helps verify that you are the rightful owner. Similar things happen in cryptocurrency transactions.

Your public address provides general information about your account, and it is essential if you want to perform any transaction. However, any transaction is unable to go through without your PIN, which in this case is your private key. The beauty of using keys is that although it is possible to generate your public key from your private key, the vice versa is impossible. Hence, your account remains secure.

Let's continue further with an example of an account number and PIN. Although a PIN is a highly secure method of identification, the system cannot identify whether it is you who has initiated the transaction. Any person in possession of your PIN is considered the rightful owner of the account by the system.

The PIN is generally just a one-step verification. And this loophole can be misused by attackers to gain access to your account. In the same manner, your private key can transfer the entire authority of ownership to the person in possession of the key.

It is essential that you do not share your private key with anyone as it grants them complete authority over your Bitcoin wallet. This can lead to significant financial losses. It is also advisable that you create a backup of your private key and store it safely. This is the only security measure that you need to follow very strictly. Otherwise the blockchain network is quite secure and intrusions are not possible unless you let hackers exploit this loophole.

How to select a cryptocurrency wallet

Prior to choosing a digital wallet, you must first learn about different types of wallets. Are you going to be a frequent user and intend to use the wallet for daily transactions or to store your Bitcoin for a long period of time? You should take this into consideration whilst selecting the crypto wallet for your needs.

There are different kinds of cryptocurrency wallets. However, you can easily classify them into two main types: online and offline. The fact of the matter is that both these wallets have different purposes. While online wallets are usually used for regular transactions, offline wallets are more like savings accounts.

The offline wallets are often called cold wallets. They are internet-disabled physical devices that occasionally require access to the Internet. You can connect them to the Internet when you need to make a transaction and then take it back to the offline world. The offline wallets are among the safest wallets to store your coins as they offer robust security and improved anti-theft protection. They are pretty much hacker-proof, you just need to make sure that it is not stolen, destroyed or wrecked. Cold wallets are cryptocurrency's alternative to a vault or a safe deposit box where you keep your long-term holdings. They are best used for storing large amounts of cryptocurrency that you don't intend to spend in the nearest future. If you are planning to invest in Bitcoin for a long term, then consider cold storage wallet.

The online wallets or 'hot' wallets are always connected to the Internet. This makes them less secure but more agile, faster and user-friendly. They give you instant access to your digital assets, wherever you are as long as you have a device connected to the Internet. But this comfort comes at a cost: they are intrinsically insecure and vulnerable to theft due to constant

Internet access. Sometimes you don't even control the security of your wallet, as it depends on the practices of your wallet service provider. Hot wallets are like a leather purse: it's perfect for petty cash to cover your everyday expenses, but you won't put all your savings in there. It's an ideal solution for keeping small amounts of cryptocurrency that you want to have at hand at any time.

Cryptocurrency offline (cold) wallets can be divided into desktop wallets, paper wallets and hardware storages. Let's take a look at these wallets:

Desktop wallets are used from your personal computer or a laptop. You are required to download the software directly onto a desktop. The wallet is downloaded for a single computer use and is accessible only from the computer on which it is installed. This kind of storage is more secure than online storages. You cannot access private keys stored on the computer from any other device. Which means it will remain on your desktop for as long as possible. You can access your Bitcoins even without connecting to the Internet. That is one major advantage. Apart from that, your Bitcoins are safe from hackers.

The only problem with this storage comes when something happens to your computer. For instance, a malware that takes all your Bitcoins away can be sent to the computer. If your hardware is hacked your coins can get copied and your Bitcoins will be transferred without your knowledge. In other words, your Bitcoins will be stolen and there is nothing you can do about it. However, if your hardware is secure this is actually one of the safer options. Besides, if you lose the computer, say it breaks down, you cannot access your wallet. The most popular examples of desktop crypto wallets are:

Exodus – an all-in-one desktop wallet that is designed in a very user-friendly way. It is perfect for those who are just starting their crypto journey. Exodus allows you to store, manage and exchange Bitcoins and a number of altcoins including Ethereum, Dash and Litecoin. It lets you track the value of your blockchain asset portfolio, in real time, whilst market conditions change. Exodus offers a very simple guide to back up your wallet. One of the great things about Exodus is that it has a built-in ShapeShift exchange that allows users to trade altcoins for Bitcoins and vice versa without leaving the wallet.

Armory – another of the most secure and advanced cold storage Bitcoin desktop wallets. It enables its users to generate and store private key data on the offline computer that never touches the Internet. Multiple backups and encryption features give you full control of your crypto assets and greatly reduce the attack attempts to steal your Bitcoins. Users are empowered with multiple encrypted Bitcoin wallets and permanent one-time 'paper backups'. Although Armory takes a little while to understand and use to its full potential, it's a great option for more experienced crypto users who are looking to keep their funds safe and secure.

The simplest wallet undoubtedly has to be the paper wallet. They are regular pieces of paper on which the private and public keys of your bitcoin address are printed. This is ideal for long-term storage or for the gifting of bitcoin to someone. These wallets are the most secure way to store your bitcoins as they're not connected to a network.

With services such as WalletGenerator.net and Bitaddress.org, you can easily create a new address and print the wallet on your printer. They are an open source random address and key generators and use your respective browser's JavaScript engine. This means that your key never goes through the channels of the Internet, making the whole procedure very safe and reliable. You can send a few coins to that address, and then store it safely or gift it to someone. All you need are your public keys. It's that simple.

The biggest advantage of the paper wallet is your keys are not accessible via the Internet and hence they are immune to any viruses or hackers. Because paper is flexible, you can store it anywhere you want. But they are so much easier to lose. This makes it worth your consideration.

You will also need to take precautions while creating the wallet. Before generating the paper, make sure no one is watching you so that you can rule out the risk of spyware too. Once the wallet is set up, ensure you are able to run offline. That way you can disconnect from the Internet before generating the keys. Lastly, use a printer that isn't connected to the network.

It is very important to understand that you are printing valuable, private information on a piece of paper. Hence, it is absolutely necessary for you to take measures to protect that piece of paper. It is recommended to keep it in a place away from water or dampness, to avoid any general wear and tear. Some people prefer laminating it and storing it in a safe, a deposit box or entrusting it to a solicitor.

Hardware wallets are a rather unique type of Bitcoin wallet. These are hardware devices similar to USB storage devices which offer the safest way to store your cryptocurrency. The user's private key is stored securely in this small hardware device. The device occasionally connects to the Internet to enact Bitcoin transactions. They are extremely secure, as they are usually offline and therefore not hackable.

The best thing about hardware storage, apart from complete security, is the fact that you can retrieve your coins if the device is lost. You don't have to worry yourself so much as long as the private key is securely stored and you have created a reliable 12 or 24 word 'recovery seed' back up for it. There have been no verifiable incidents of money being stolen from a hardware wallet. Not just that, they are immune to computer viruses as nothing can be transferred in plain text and in most cases, their software is open sourced.

The hardware wallet is the safest option to store your Bitcoins. However, you must keep the hardware wallet in a safe and secure place. Taking risks with your wallet and being careless with your private keys are some of the major reasons why people lose out. This is why some large investors have chosen to keep their hardware wallets in secure locations such as bank vaults.

Unlike paper wallets that need to be imported to software at some point, hardware wallets can be used safely. As long as you invest in an authentic device made by a trustworthy, competent manufacturer with a good reputation, your coins will be safe and secure. Trezor, KeepKey and Ledger are some notable examples of offline hardware wallets. There are varying differences among these hardware devices. The most noticeable difference involves features. There are some with great display features allowing you to use it even without connecting to the computer. Consider such features when making your selection.

KeepKey is a simple and secure multi-currency hardware wallet with advanced features. It generates a private key using a hardware-based random number generator, combined with randomness provided by your computer. Once your private key is generated, you are given the one-time opportunity to write down a backup of your KeepKey in the form of a twelve-word recovery sentence.

The wallet supports Bitcoin, Bitcoin Cash, Ethereum, Litecoin, Dash, and multiple Ethereum-based tokens. This makes the wallet perfect for if you are using a variety of cryptocurrencies or looking to build a diversified portfolio of digital assets. KeepKey is one of the most secure environments for storing your cryptocurrency.

Trezor is another cryptocurrency hardware wallet which is perfect for individuals who want to protect their investments with extra layer of security. Both models Trezor One and Trezor T can handle over 500 cryptocurrencies which include Bitcoin, Ethereum, Litecoin, Dash, ZCash and others. If you need a wallet that handles even more digital currencies, then you are better off going with the Model T. Both models are very user-friendly devices and are simple to use. Trezor has developed an online software which you will have to download to be able connect your wallet to and set it up. Trezor is and has been at the front of hardware-based cryptocurrency wallets. No matter whether you choose Trezor T or Trezor One, you will get a wallet that will guarantee the safety of your digital assets.

Ledger Nano S is considered to be most universal cryptocurrency hardware wallet. It's simple to use and an incredibly secure wallet. It is protected within a guarded secure chip, the same kind that is used for passports and credit cards. The Ledger Nano S supports more than 30 cryptocurrencies including Bitcoin, Ethereum, Ripple, Litecoin, ERC20 tokens, and Dash among others. You will be required to download the Ledger Live Software application on your computer which is needed to manage, send and receive your Bitcoins or altcoins. The Ledger company has launched the even more secure and advanced cryptocurrency wallets Ledger Blue and Ledger Nano X. Their features include compatibility with a huge range of devices, user-friendly interface, multiple currency support and most importantly, the highest level of security for your coins.

Now, if you consider using cryptocurrency for frequent transactions or daily trading then hot wallets will suit you better. There are mainly three types of hot wallets from which you can choose, a cloud web-based wallet, a mobile and an exchange-based version. Although this may sound simple, each of these wallets has different purposes, different levels of security and different functions.

Your browser wallet or your web-based wallet runs on the cloud and is convenient as you can access it from almost any computer in any location. However, it is not as secure as the other options since your keys are controlled by a third party. This makes them more vulnerable to hacking attacks and theft. Of course, no wallet service provider wants to be hacked, but that is not something that is under your or their control. In fact, using this wallet is ironic as the entire purpose of creating a cryptocurrency was to keep your funds under only your control.

So the entire purpose of using cryptocurrency is defeated here. But it cannot be denied that this option is very convenient especially since your wallet provider usually allows you to purchase coins through their online service. If you do still feel that you need to use this option, choose a provider that encrypts the keys before putting them on the web, thus making this option relatively safe and secure.

If you are considering using a web-based cryptocurrency wallet then you should create one by installing MetaMask. MetaMask is a free and secure extension for many popular browsers like Chrome, Firefox, Opera and Brave that allows web applications to read and interact with the Ethereum blockchain. Once MetaMask extension is installed, you can create a cryptocurrency wallet to store, send and receive ERC20 tokens based on Ethereum protocol. It is one of the top web digital wallets with a simple and clear user-friendly interface.

MyEtherWallet is another web wallet that allows its users to send and receive Ethereum and Ethereum-based (ERC20) tokens. It doesn't support Bitcoin, Litecoin, or other related currencies. MyEtherWallet is an open-source wallet that interacts directly with Ethereum blockchain without having to join any centralized exchange. The wallet doesn't store your private keys or any information on its servers, which means the user is in complete control of their own security and privacy.

Mobile cryptocurrency wallets run on an app on your phone and are useful because they can be used anywhere including retail stores. Mobile wallets are usually much smaller and simpler than desktop wallets because of the limited space available on a mobile.

While being convenient, mobile crypto wallets create a unique set of potential security vulnerabilities. First, phones are often lost or misplaced. Additionally, if the wallet key is only stored on the phone, a broken or lost phone can become a much more expensive mishap, possibly making your wallet permanently inaccessible. As a third consideration, a mobile wallet provides more ways to pinpoint your identity, by potentially exposing your phone number, wallet key or address, and your geolocation.

If you choose to use a mobile wallet, consider limiting the amount of currency you store in that wallet and keeping the main balance of your cryptocurrency in a more secure hardware wallet.

Mobile wallets are very practical as you can easily use them in retail stores to pay for goods and services. Nowadays, there are many mobile wallets available on the market with different cryptographic security features for storing your digital coins. However, they are vulnerable to cyber threats, viruses and malware as they are always connected to the Internet. Hence, you have to be extra careful and do your own thorough research before choosing a reliable and secure wallet.

The blockchain claims to be the first and most trusted global cryptocurrency company. It developed the world's safest and most popular Bitcoin mobile wallet for investing and storing your digital assets. Accessing this wallet can also be done from any browser. For the browser version, users can enable 2FA authentication, while mobile users can activate a pin code requirement every time the wallet application is opened. It will allow you to store and transact Bitcoin, Ethereum, Stellar and Bitcoin Cash using the best security and safety features of the cryptocurrency wallet. Furthermore, it enables its users to exchange one crypto for another without ever leaving the blockchain wallet. Although your wallet will be stored online and all transactions will need to go through the company's servers, Blockchain.info does not have access to your private keys. Overall, this is a well-established company that is trusted throughout the Bitcoin community and makes for a solid wallet to keep your currency.

Jaxx is another multi-currency wallet which supports nearly 70 cryptocurrencies including Bitcoin, Litecoin, ZCash, Ethereum and many

ERC20 tokens. As well as apps for iOS and Android, you can access Jaxx from your desktop or tablet with a dedicated client for Windows, Mac or Linux. Chrome and Firefox extensions also bring a limited feature set to the leading web browsers. Integration with ShapeShift service allows you to exchange cryptocurrencies right from the wallet and re-balance your portfolio as desired. It has a simple and attractive user interface which is easy to use. Jaxx wallet offers a client-side security model meaning that it doesn't hold onto your crypto funds and you are in control of your private keys. Moreover, it uses standards that ensure your keys can be imported into another service, should the company cease to exist.

Advanced users searching for a Bitcoin mobile digital wallet should look no further than the **Mycelium** wallet. The Mycelium mobile wallet allows iPhone and Android users to store, send and receive Bitcoins. Moreover, it allows its users to buy and sell Bitcoin in exchange for fiat currency (US dollars, Euros, etc). All of this can be done on one account or multiple accounts that have enterprise-level security features like cold storage and encrypted PDF backups. The wallet has been recognized as one of the best mobile wallets in the Bitcoin industry, so much so that it was awarded the 2014 Best Mobile App by Blockchain.info.

Cryptocurrency exchanges are web-based platforms or services that let you to convert your fiat currency like, US Dollars, Euro etc., to a cryptocurrency of your choice and convert the coins back into fiat currency as either your original currency or any other currency of your choice. In other words, a cryptocurrency exchange is a platform which allows you to buy, sell or even trade Bitcoin for other cryptocurrencies or traditional currency. The exchange is an intermediary between buyers and sellers. Almost everyone will want to use an exchange due to its convenience. If exchanges didn't exist, you would have to buy your coins from somebody who already owns them, only after agreeing on a rate. The same goes for selling your coins. You would have to find someone who wanted to buy them and then agree on a price. Exchanges simplify the process by providing a place to buy and sell your coins.

Exchange-based wallets are suitable for cryptocurrency traders who use exchanges as both an exchange and a crypto wallet. Although they are made convenient for buying, selling, or trading cryptocurrencies through the exchange platforms, these are very risky. Due to an increasing number of hacking attacks on exchanges, it has been proven that they are the most vulnerable places to store your Bitcoins.

Therefore, it's usually not recommended to use an exchange or its remote wallet as a place to store significant amounts of cryptocurrency. One strategy to help manage risk is to keep smaller amounts of currency in exchanges or other less-secure locations or platforms that make a more attractive target for hackers or other impropriety.

Exchanges like Coinbase, Kraken, Bittrex, and Binance are the biggest in the field and among the most reliable crypto exchanges. The concern is that the exchanges hold your private keys, implying that it is like storing your coins in their wallet. It requires you to place a lot of trust in the exchange. That is why it is recommended to use the services of big names in the market like Coinbase or Kraken as they have a decent track record in comparison with other smaller exchanges that may not be as trustworthy. However, diligent security precautions still need to be implemented and followed when using this type of wallet.

Bitcoin has brought into existence hundreds of alternative cryptocurrencies, each with their own distinctive ecosystem and infrastructure. Hence, these days many cryptocurrency holders own more than one kind of cryptocurrency. Maintaining a separate wallet for each type of currency can be very tedious work. If you are interested in buying only a single digital currency, like Bitcoin, then you will need to set up a currency specific wallet. This wallet will support a single currency which means that you can send and receive only compatible cryptocurrency. For example, if you attempt to send Bitcoins to an Ethereum wallet, the chances are that your funds will be lost forever.

If you don't want to limit yourself to a single cryptocurrency, then it may be more convenient to set up a multi-currency wallet. These wallets are designed to hold more than one coin and enable you to use several currencies from the same wallet. However, some popular cryptocurrencies are not well-supported by current multi-currency wallet options, which create a need for a separate single wallet for these currencies.

Choosing the best cryptocurrency wallet is highly dependent on what your specific needs are and your thoughts on security versus convenience or hardware vs software.

After you have learnt about the types of cryptocurrency wallets, the next step is to understand how to select a secure and trusted wallet. When choosing one, always remember that it is your responsibility to perform research carefully and consider the following:

-        Use only trusted wallets with a proven reputation and stay away from little-known no-name companies.

-       Install software only from trusted sources and don't use wallets unless you are 100% sure it's a valid software. Some wallets are not that innocent as they are created with the sole purpose to steal your crypto assets.

-       Check the reviews about secure wallets and try to find someone among your friends who uses these wallets.

-       Also, don't forget to analyze the development team behind the wallet.

-       Give preference to non-third party wallets that will let you to have full control of your private keys.

-       Get the download link from the official website of the wallet as both the App Store and Google Play are plagued with fake wallets. Ensure that the web address in the URL field has correct spelling and doesn't include any apostrophe or underscore etc. symbols.

-       Check a wallet on https://bitcoin.org/en/choose-your-wallet before downloading. From there you can select a secure wallet of any type: hardware, desktop, mobile or web.

Although some cryptocurrency wallets are more secure than the others by their nature, their level of security is still limited to a varying degree. Quite often crypto wallets are exposed to possible vulnerabilities such as hacking attacks, malware or simply users are not taking any safety precautions to protect their wallets. Hence, you should always implement security features and follow them when using any wallet. Here are some steps you can take to ensure the best safety for your wallets:

-       Creating backups to remain on the safe side in case the device or data gets lost is always favorable. For that, you have to back up your entire wallet to protect it against computer failures, malware and human error. By doing so you can recover your stolen wallet if it is encrypted. Therefore, you must always keep an offline backup of your private keys at a location that only you know and trust. It is better done on an offline device, such as a USB drive, as online storage can be hacked or compromised. You should also keep backup copies of your mnemonic phrases, passwords, PIN codes, usernames and other access data in two different places. Just in case it has been long enough for you to forget these things, you will have a source to refer to if you have their backups.

-       By encrypting your wallet, you add additional layers of security. You can do so by encrypting your wallet using a passphrase. This passphrase will allow you to lock your coins. This makes it difficult for the hackers to take anything unless they know your passphrase. If you are using a mobile device or a laptop to do the transaction, then encrypting your wallet becomes absolutely essential as you are almost always connected to the Internet.

-       Adding extra security layers. The more layers of security, the better. Setting strong passwords and usernames, ensuring any withdrawal of funds requires a password is a start. Use wallets that provide extra security layers like two-factor authentication and additional pin code

 requirements every time a wallet application is opened.

-       Software updates are among the most common and easiest security measures to protect your wallet from new threats. You must always use the latest version of the software irrespective of which wallet you are using. The updated software will keep you informed about the latest security fixes, thus safeguarding your wallet. You should regularly update not only your wallet software but also the antivirus and anti-malware software on your computer or mobile. Additionally, install a strong and secure firewall.

- Keep small amounts of cryptocurrencies for everyday expenses in a hot wallet, online or on mobile and store the majority of your cryptocurrency funds in a secure place in a cold wallet away from Internet access. A hardware or paper wallet will protect your money from hackers, malware and viruses and allow you to recover data if your computer or mobile device dies.

- Applying safe practices when using the wallet. Always double check the address where you send your digital money to and never access the wallet from a public Wi-Fi.

By doing all this you can be assured that your crypto wallet is secure. Always remember that it is your responsibility to protect your investments in digital assets. When you have done research and selected the most appropriate wallet you would like to use, the next step is to set it up and get it ready for your first Bitcoin purchase.

Being new to the cryptocurrency world, you might want to start buying a small amount of Bitcoin or any other cryptocurrency. Hence, you should consider installing a free online-based hot wallet for your desktop or smartphone. It is very easy to create a cryptocurrency wallet and the whole process doesn't require a lot of time. Below you will find a guide that will help you create a digital wallet on your desktop or smartphone:

Step 1: Do the research and select the most appropriate wallet that will keep your digital money safe. Before choosing the wallet you have to consider the following major criteria: safety level, reputation, available assets, user-friendly interface and convenience.

Step 2: Once you have selected the wallet, you will need to go to a market App on your smartphone or Google web browser on your PC and search for the wallet application or the site link.

Step 3: After you have downloaded the correct software/application, follow the on-screen instructions to install it.

Step 4: Complete the installation process and go to the Main Menu. Then click on the button 'Create new wallet'.

Step 5: Generally, for most online wallets you have to follow the registration steps and verify your wallet. You will be required to enter your email address and create a strong password and a pin code. You should receive the confirmation email to be able to verify your wallet. Click on the provided link and your first new wallet is successfully created.

Step 6: Before you use the wallet, access the 'Settings' where you can change your personal preferences.

Step 7: Then go to 'Backup' option in the menu and create a backup for your wallet by setting the recovery options in emergency situations. Write down on a piece of paper the backup 12-word seed phrase in the correct order. Then store it safely in a place that is accessible only by you.

Step 8: The next step is to write down your private key and password/pin. Keep this information safe and never share it with anyone.

Step 9: In most cases, you have to activate your desktop wallet first to be able to use it. Hence, you will have to buy or transfer some cryptocurrency to the wallet address (example:qzdh0kdpp28ptv4dqqlg0n9nj2xp5672dyp0 dtkcn0). After you receive the funds, your new wallet is activated and ready for use.

Now that you know how to create your new cryptocurrency wallet, it is time to acquire your first Bitcoin. There are several ways that you can use to buy Bitcoin or any other cryptocurrency. The most common way to buy Bitcoin is directly from other people via peer-to-peer (P2P) market places, ATMs or cryptocurrency exchange trading platforms. Alternatively, if you are running a business, you can accept cryptocurrency for goods or services that you offer.

P2P Bitcoin market

The best way to buy cryptocurrency is through a peer-to-peer trading platform LocalBitcoins.com. It is quite similar to other traditional online market places where you buy any other products or services. At LocalBitcoins you can find people near you who are willing to exchange their Bitcoins for local currency. On this platform sellers or buyers post advertisements where they state exchange rate and payment methods for buying or selling cryptocurrency. Once you find the right seller, you can agree to meet the person to buy Bitcoin for cash, or trade directly with online banking. Bitcoins are placed in LocalBitcoins.com web wallet from where you can pay your Bitcoin purchases directly. Then you can transfer your first Bitcoin to your personal cryptocurrency wallet.

You will need to register with LocalBitcoins.com to proceed with the purchase. The registration process is very simple and won't take you more than a couple of minutes. You will be asked to provide a standard set of personal data: username, email and password. Don't forget to verify your email by clicking the link in the confirmation letter. Additionally, the service will ask you to provide your real name and verify your identity before you can search for the best offers from the sellers in your neighborhood.

P2P platforms are the fastest and easiest way to buy Bitcoin. However, this comfort comes at a price: the exchange rate at such places is usually higher and sometimes additional fees apply.

Bitcoin ATM

You can also use a Bitcoin ATM to buy your first fraction of Bitcoin. They are one of the easiest and quickest ways to buy and sell Bitcoins. Bitcoin ATMs work like a regular ATM, except they allow you to deposit and withdraw money so you can buy or sell virtual money. Coin ATM Radar has an interactive map to help you find the closest Bitcoin ATM near you. Download the mobile app or website page and find where to buy or sell Bitcoins, and other digital currencies for cash.

Recently, the network of Bitcoin ATMs around the globe has seen a dramatic rise. According to research, there are now 4,380 ATMs in the world that support Bitcoin (BTC). Litecoin (LTC) has seen the biggest growth in support in 2019, with a total of 2,895 ATMs now supporting LTC. There are a total of 3,095 crypto ATMs worldwide that support other altcoins. Therefore, you can easily purchase any cryptocurrency from the local Bitcoin ATM and send it directly to your mobile or even a hardware crypto wallet.

Cryptocurrency exchange

Another of the easiest and most popular ways to get cryptocurrency is to look for a trusted cryptocurrency exchange in your local geographical area. A cryptocurrency exchange is an intermediary that creates a convenient infrastructure for buying and selling digital currencies. Choose a reputable crypto exchange and ensure that it supports cryptocurrency you wish to invest money in. There are many exchanges where you may buy or sell Bitcoins for fiat money (GBP, US dollar, Euro or your local currency), though they offer different services in terms of reliability, liquidity or security. Whilst choosing an exchange, don't forget to take into account such parameters as user-friendliness of the interface, technical support, trading volume, purchase and withdrawal limits, small spread and low trading fees.

Hopefully, you have become familiar with the cryptocurrency world and already acquired your first Bitcoin. If you decide to hold Bitcoins as a long-term investment, then you should consider (without any doubt) keeping your digital assets on an offline hardware wallet. Those who are interested in the short-term investment strategy and may want to trade cryptocurrencies to make extra money over time will need to register with a cryptocurrency exchange. For a beginner, it is the most convenient place to exchange conventional fiat money for cryptocurrency. You can keep your crypto funds in an automatically generated wallet on the exchange and trade them later at a higher price.

Currently, there are hundreds of cryptocurrency exchanges operating worldwide. And, just like with crypto wallets, these too will require thorough research on your end before choosing the right one. You may be lucky and have some reputable exchanges to select from or you may even be limited to one or two based on your geographical area. When you choose cryptocurrency exchanges, you need to ensure that they have built-in security measures to protect your funds from any theft threats. Situations where cryptocurrency traders lose their money due to the exchange being hacked happens on a regular basis. There are also some cases where exchanges suddenly terminate their operations with little explanation, leading to the complete loss of funds by investors. So it is crucial to choose a trusted exchange.

In the beginning, it is a good idea to go with the biggest and most well-known exchanges like Coinbase, Kraken, Binance, Bittrex, and Poloniex and a few others. These are considered to be the most popular crypto exchanges with the highest levels of customer protection in the world. Let's take a look at the most trusted international cryptocurrency exchanges that offer a high level of customer protection.

Coinbase

Used by millions of trusted investors globally, Coinbase is one of the most popular and largest cryptocurrency brokers and trading platforms in the world. Founded in June 2012, the San Francisco-based cryptocurrency exchange is available to users in over 55 countries.

The Coinbase platform makes it easy to securely buy, use and store digital currencies like Bitcoin, Bitcoin Cash, Ethereum, Ethereum Classic, and Litecoin. Moreover, Coinbase recently launched a direct crypto-to crypto trading feature. Millions of Coinbase customers can now trade between different cryptocurrencies including XRP, EOS, Stellar, 0x, Basic Attention

Token, ZCash and others.

Customers can sign up and buy Bitcoin and other cryptocurrencies through a digital wallet available on Coinbase.com and download its iOS and Android mobile applications. Alternatively they can also sign up for a Coinbase Pro account to be able to access advanced cryptocurrency to cryptocurrency trading options. In both cases users must provide personal details and go through the full identity verification process before first-time buyers will be able to purchase Bitcoins.

Coinbase is a beginner friendly exchange that provides convenience to all its users. Furthermore, Coinbase's dashboard has exceptionally simple features and its interface is easy to use. Customers can buy Bitcoin with a connected bank account or SEPA transfer, debit or credit card, or PayPal payment method. They can also use the facility of instant exchange by converting digital currency to local currency immediately. The Coinbase platform offers its users the dollar-cost averaging option to invest automatically with recurring purchases at regular intervals.

Additionally, Coinbase exchange has introduced 'Coinbase Earn', an educational content option to its customers. It allows users to earn cryptocurrencies, while learning about them in a simple and engaging way. The idea is for users to go to the 'Coinbase Earn' page to earn small amounts of cryptocurrencies by completing educational tasks like short video lessons and quizzes.

Coinbase recently launched a Visa debit Coinbase card that is available in the UK and six European countries. These countries include Spain, Germany, France, Italy, Ireland and the Netherlands. The Coinbase card will be funded by the individual's Coinbase balance and will allow customers to spend their cryptocurrency worldwide for everyday shopping activities. Coinbase also promised that in the near future they will be introducing some new features and will also bring the card to more customers on a global level.

You can always rely on Coinbase when it comes to security of your crypto funds. Their website servers have SSL encryption. Most of the currency is stored offline to add an extra layer of protection. The platform also has a multi-signature vault that controls all private keys during transactions. Both wallets and keys are covered under AES-256 encryption. The currency is distributed all over in wallets and vaults to make it more protective and less accessible. Coinbase also provides insurance for the digital coins since they store cryptocurrencies on the servers. Insurance policies come as blessings and also makes the platform more reliable, especially due to increased cyber-criminal activities. If you wish to add additional security, then you can enable 2FA two-step verification for your account.

Coinbase is the world's largest exchange and has been around since the early days of Bitcoin. It is one of the most popular and reliable cryptocurrency platforms that offers easy ways for new users to buy Bitcoin. There is no doubt that the well-known cryptocurrency exchange greatly helps the adoption of cryptocurrencies worldwide.

Kraken

Founded in 2011, Kraken is one of the oldest Bitcoin exchanges on the market. Just like Coinbase, the exchange is also headquartered in San Francisco. Over the years, it has become the largest Bitcoin exchange in euro volume and liquidity. Kraken also supports fiat currencies such as Canadian dollars, US dollars, British pounds and Japanese yen. Fiat deposits and withdrawals are completed through SEPA, Swift and bank wires. Credit cards, debit cards and PayPal are not currently supported.

Kraken is consistently being reported as the best and most secure Bitcoin exchange by independent news media. In fact, it was the first Bitcoin exchange platform to have the trading price and volume displayed on the Bloomberg Terminal. Kraken is currently the 11th largest among the other cryptocurrency exchanges in the world by daily trade volumes. Today, Kraken is trusted by government officials in Japan and regulated banks throughout Europe, making it one of the most respected exchanges available.

The exchange platform offers an increasingly wide range of high-volume digital currencies. The cryptocurrencies that are available for trading include Bitcoin, Etherum, XRP, Bitcoin Cash, Stellar, Dash, Litecoin, Monero, ZCash, EOS, Ethereum Classic and many other.

Kraken is a very popular platform among intermediate users or professional crypto traders. The user interface is not as beginner friendly as other exchanges like Coinbase. However, once you study the platform's features, it is not that difficult to use it. Compared to other beginner-friendly exchanges, Kraken offers free deposits for Euro, Canadian dollar and Japanese yen and very low trading fees.

The platform offers comprehensive services such as the ability to buy and sell cryptocurrencies and trade them against fiat currencies or Bitcoin. It also provides access to advanced features such as fast execution speed, margin trading and deep liquidity.

Signing up for an account on Kraken is similar to creating an account on most cryptocurrency exchanges. The registration process takes between five and ten minutes and is easy to follow. The exchange has included extra security features on the sign up page to secure and protect user accounts. The platform also meets Know Your Customer (KYC) and Anti-Money Laundering (AML) requirements from regulators. Additionally, users have the option to create a master key that gives their accounts a second layer of security. This is especially useful when changing password or switching to a new mobile or PC device.

Kraken is one of the safest Bitcoin exchanges which offers a high level of security. The platform provides cryptography-verified proof of reserve audits. These audits verify the total amount of cryptocurrency held by Kraken. Furthermore, all new deposits go directly to cold wallets, where most of the coins are stored. Kraken's exchange uses cryptography tools to encrypt all active wallets, account information and verification documents. Users also enjoy two-factor authentication and other security measures that help to protect personal login details against malicious attempts.

If you are keen on using Kraken's exchange, simply visit the website Kraken.com and open an account to get started. You will be prompted to complete registration and activate your account. Once verified, you can deposit fiat currency or transfer cryptocurrency from another exchange to your account.

Binance

Launched in July 2017, the Hong Kong-based Binance exchange is considered the biggest cryptocurrency exchange in the world in terms of trading volume. It is one of the most popular exchanges that provides a platform for trading more than 100 cryptocurrencies supported for deposit and withdrawal. Binance is a crypto-to-crypto only trading platform that offers the easiest and cheapest way to exchange Bitcoin, Ethereum, Litecoin, Binance coin for other digital currencies and tokens.

Besides trading, you can use Binance exchange to expand your cryptocurrency portfolio and include other promising altcoins for future gains. Most cryptocurrency exchanges are limited to only a few coins whilst Binance offers the widest selection of cryptocurrencies and tokens in the market. Hence, you can transfer Bitcoin, Ethereum or Litecoin to your Binance account first and then buy other cryptocurrencies for your diversified portfolio. It is suggested to use Litecoin for transfers between exchanges as it has low transaction fees compared to others.

The Binance company was initially founded in China. In September 2017, it relocated its headquarters into Japan in advance of the Chinese government ban on cryptocurrency trading. In March 2018, after stricter regulations in Japan, Binance had to move an office to the crypto-friendly Malta. In 2019, the company established Binance Jersey, an independent entity from its parent Binance.com exchange with the aim to expand its influence in Europe. The Jersey based exchange offers fiat-to cryptocurrency pairs, including Euro and the British pound. In January 2019, Binance has partnered with payment processor Simplex to allow six different cryptocurrency purchases with debit and credit cards, such as Visa and

Mastercard. However, this service comes with a premium fee of 3.5%. There is no fee charged for cryptocurrency fund deposits, though withdrawals come with a transaction fee that varies depending upon the cryptocurrency.

Binance is famous for its low trading fees, high liquidity and fast transaction processing. The Binance technology is capable of processing 1.4 million orders every second, and thus making Binance one of the fastest exchanges in the market. The exchange platform has the largest volume of trading cryptocurrency pairs in Bitcoin, Ethereum and USDT markets.

In addition, it offers the native BNB cryptocurrency tokens which can be used to trade cryptocurrencies, pay for fees and participate in Initial Coin Offerings. Launched in July 2017, Binance Coin (BNB) has gained popularity and is actively traded with a market capitalization of around $4.4 billion as of August 2019. BNB provides an additional 25% discount on the trade fee to its users when trading with the coin.

Binance provides standard exchange services around trading, listing, funding and withdrawal of
cryptocurrencies. In addition, Binance offers other services for supporting the blockchain ecosystem. Thus, a blockchain technology incubator called Binance Labs helps cryptocurrency project teams to raise funds for development and launch of their own tokens. Binance also runs Initial Coin Offering listings for emerging blockchain projects on its token launch platform Launchpad.

The platform offers two options for digital currency trading: basic and advanced. If you are new to trading, you might experience difficulty using the platform for the first time. However, anyone with a background in digital currencies and with a bit of knowledge into how exchanges work should be able to use the platform and its different services.

The basic view has all the user needs to execute simple trades. The dashboard for the basic version offers several graphs and charts for the pairs that you are trading, order books and trade history. The advanced view is for more advanced traders who are able to do more in-depth technical analysis of digital currency value over time. Hence, it gives users access to advanced charting tools. Platform users can easily choose between the basic and advanced interfaces.

To use Binance exchange, users will have to create an account. The process behind it is very simple and users don't have to verify their ID for Level 1, which has a daily withdrawal limit up to two Bitcoins. However, for higher limits, users have to complete the necessary KYC requirements and wait for ID approval. Once the account is verified, they can add cryptocurrency funds to the public wallet address provided by Binance and start buying or trading other cryptocurrencies.

Binance is considered a safe exchange that allows user account protection via the use of 2FA authentication. It claims high standards of safety and security with multi-tier and multi-clustered architecture. Furthermore, it has taken many steps to earn a high level of trust from its users and the crypto community. However, the best practice is to keep small amounts of cryptocurrency on exchanges and move the rest into a cold storage hardware wallet.

If you are still not sure how to choose a secure crypto exchange, then you should go to www.bitcoin.org and at the top of home page click on 'resources/exchanges' for a full list of international Bitcoin exchanges. Alternatively, you can find a lot of information about exchange trading platforms on www.Coinmarketcap.com.

There are many exchanges that offer a wide range of cryptocurrency pairs and trading services. They will allow you to buy various cryptocurrencies and diversify your trading portfolio. Moreover, you can take advantage of opportunities offered by less popular cheap altcoins. While smaller exchanges might tempt you with favorable trading conditions, large and well established companies offer higher trading volumes and lower trading fees. Hence, you will be able to buy and sell any amount of digital currency with minimal costs.

It is important to note that not all crypto exchanges accept traditional money. Some exchanges allow you to deposit only Bitcoin to purchase other alternative coins. Bitcoin is the leading cryptocurrency that you can buy on almost all crypto exchanges. Thus, you may have to buy Bitcoin somewhere else first and then transfer it into the exchange where you can start buying and trading any other alternative currencies.

If you are new to cryptocurrencies, then your first step will be to find the way that allows you to convert your local currency into Bitcoin. Hence, you should find an ATM or exchange in your domestic country to convert money from your bank account into Bitcoin. In other words, if you want to buy Bitcoin through your local cryptocurrency exchange, you must do the following:

Step 1: Open a domestic cryptocurrency exchange in your country and verify your account (submit identity proof).

Step 2: Deposit funds from your bank account to your crypto exchange account and start buying Bitcoin.

Step 3: Open a crypto exchange account that offers a variety of other coins. Usually these exchanges do not accept fiat deposits and only allow coin deposits.

Step 4: After verifying your account, transfer the Bitcoin that you've bought from your local exchange to your new crypto exchange and you can start buying other coins with your Bitcoin.

However, most popular international exchanges like Coinbase or Kraken accept payments via bank transfer or credit card. And some are even willing to work with PayPal transfers. They charge fees which in most cases are different between crypto exchanges and include the cost for using the Bitcoin network. So after the exchange receives payment from you, the corresponding amount of Bitcoin will be purchased on your behalf.

You should always remember that cryptocurrency exchanges are not regulated entities. It means that they do not have an oversight authority that controls their actions or protects traders from bad actors, manipulations and malpractices. Cryptocurrency traders have to be extra vigilant while choosing a cryptocurrency trading platform and consider the following:

1. Cryptocurrency pair available
Many exchanges offer only a few cryptocurrencies such as Bitcoin, Ethereum, Bitcoin Cash or Litecoin. There are only a handful of

exchanges that offer a wider variety of coins. A more diverse option of cryptocurrencies is better as it gives you more choices to diversify your portfolio.

2. Higher liquidity

Liquidity refers to the ease of buying and selling assets in the market. A high liquidity means that there is a large number of buyers and sellers to trade with. High liquidity leads to a better price determination and it allows you to transact faster.

3. High level of security

The level and type of security measures implemented by an exchange is very important in ensuring that your crypto funds are safe. Examples of good security practices undertaken by exchanges include availability of the two-factor authentication (2FA) option which increases the security of your account; email encryption and verification that enables emails sent to your account to confirm every transaction; keeping deposits in cold offline storage which means that your coins are safely stored away from the reach of hackers.

4. Trading fees

Low transaction fees on buying and selling would prevent your margins being taken away, especially if you are full-time trader. It is important to compare the fees across different exchanges.

5. User friendly interface

The user interface of exchange should be clear, intuitive and user-friendly to avoid any confusion. Having the ease of navigating through the platform's dashboard options should make it easy for new beginners to set up an account and purchase Bitcoin with only a few clicks.

6. Customer Support Quality

Having a responsive customer and technical support would save you a lot of time and money when dealing with issues on your verification process, deposits and withdrawals, funds reflection and trading orders. Cryptocurrency exchanges should be reliable and resolve these and many other issues fairly quickly.

7. Good track of hackerproof history

If your cryptocurrency exchange is hacked, you are likely to lose all your crypto assets and there will be no one held responsible or to compensate your losses. This means that you are in charge of your finances to the full extent when choosing a reliable crypto exchange. Hence, in order to reduce the chances of your assets being stolen by hackers, you should check if the exchange of your choice hasn't been the target of a hacking attack incident in the past. Using a cryptocurrency exchange with a good track of hackerproof history is essential to prevent investors from suffering serious financial losses.

Registering with a cryptocurrency exchange

The next step is to register and open an account with a cryptocurrency trading exchange, deposit some funds and then start buying and selling Bitcoin and other cryptocurrencies.

All cryptocurrency exchanges offer a simple registration procedure, though most of them require ID verification under Anti Money Laundering (AML) or Know Your Customer (KYC) regulations. You will need to provide basic personal identity information and create an account at exchange without having to buy Bitcoin at that time. The confirmation may take a while, so it is better to initiate the registration process well in advance.

Although the registration process will vary depending on the cryptocurrency exchange you sign up to, you should go through the same steps:

Step 1: Download the web page of your chosen cryptocurrency exchange and go to sign up/register for a user account.

Step 2: On the registration page you will have to enter your name, email address and set a password. Once all the details are provided, submit the form by hitting the 'Create Account' or 'Register' button.

Step 3: After submitting the form, you will be sent a verification email to the email address that you provided during signup. Go to the inbox of your email and check for an email from an exchange, and verify your account.

Step 4: After you have verified your email, your account will be created. In order to start buying Bitcoin, you will need to set your 2-step verification method and confirm your mobile number. To do this, provide your mobile number and you will receive a text code. Enter this code on the exchange website and click on 'Continue'. Mobile number verification is required as a part of your login process. Moreover, it is a recommended security measure for all your future transactions.

Alternatively, you can select another way of verification called authentication method. For this you will need to download the Google Authenticator application on your smartphone. Every time you need to access your exchange account or perform a transaction, you will be asked to type a one-time based 6-digit code generated by your authenticator.

Step 5: The next important step is to verify your identity before you can actually purchase the cryptocurrency. Upload a copy of your passport and/ or driving license and go through the simple steps of KYC verification. The whole process will take only a couple of minutes after which you will be able to buy your first Bitcoin.

Step 6: There are two different options to deposit money and fund your Bitcoin account. Funding with your bank account will enable you to buy a higher amount of Bitcoin but can take a few working days. Buying with a debit or credit card will give you a lower limit but you can get all your coins instantly. However, bear in mind the higher transaction fees.

Step 7: In order to get your first Bitcoin or Ethereum you will have to verify your bank account details. Alternatively you can verify your credit or debit card should you use it as another payment option. All you have to do is follow the on-screen instructions and verify two pending transactions on your bank account or credit card. Simply enter these two amounts back into the cryptocurrency exchange funding page. Thus, you have added your bank account or credit card as a payment method and are ready to buy your first Bitcoin!

How to buy or sell Bitcoin with a cryptocurrency exchange

Once you have added funds to your cryptocurrency exchange account, you will be able to start making transactions on the platform and buy your first Bitcoin. If you are just getting started then you should definitely stick to a user friendly and reliable cryptocurrency exchange for beginners. Buying Bitcoin on an exchange like Coinbase is very simple.

Coinbase is a popular name in the world of cryptocurrencies and is a digital multi-currency exchange in operation since 2012. It serves 32 countries and supports fiat currencies such as USD, EUR and GBP. Apart from Bitcoin, you can also buy Ethereum, Litecoin, Bitcoin Cash and Ethereum Classic there.

Since Coinbase happens to be one of the widely used exchanges amongst beginners, given below are the steps through which you can buy Bitcoins using their platform. Just follow these few simple steps:

Step 1: Once you are logged in to your Coinbase account, you will need to go to your Dashboard page.

Step 2: Click on the 'Buy/Sell' button at the top and choose the cryptocurrency that you wish to purchase.

Step 3: Choose your USD, GBP or Euro wallet as your payment option from the drop-down menu.

Step 4: Enter the amount of money that you wish to spend on this purchase. Alternatively, you can enter the amount of cryptocurrency that you wish to buy.

Step 5: Before clicking on 'Buy Bitcoin instantly', Coinbase will provide you with details of Coinbase fees and the total amount spent.

Step 6: Once you are happy with the fees, click on 'Buy Bitcoin instantly'.

Congratulations! You have purchased your first Bitcoin!

Furthermore, you can set up reoccurring buys on a daily, weekly or yearly basis. Thus, it will allow you to increase your investment over time.

Coinbase exchange offers two different ways for you to buy cryptocurrency. With the bank account option you will have to transfer the money from your bank account first. And then you will have to wait a few days for your transfer to go through before you can purchase Bitcoin. However, if you need to buy cryptocurrency instantly, you can use a credit card as the second option.

Bank account option

If you choose to buy Bitcoins using this option, you need to have some money deposited in your Coinbase account. You can do so by following the steps given below:

Step 1: First of all, go to your Coinbase account page and click on the 'Account' button. After that select GBP, Euro or USD wallet depending on the currency that you wish to deposit.

Step 2: Click on the 'Deposit' button and copy the reference number given by Coinbase.

Step 3: Open your registered bank account and initiate a transaction to Coinbase's bank account as per the details provided by them.

Step 4: Once you have completed the transfer, go back to your Coinbase account and click on 'I've sent the funds'.

Remember, this transfer does take some time to reflect in your account as Coinbase has to verify the transfer to your account. Usually, this takes 2–3 days.

A standard fee of 1.49% is levied if you are transferring the funds to or from your USD wallet at US$201 and above. Once your transfer goes through, you can use these funds to buy any of the cryptocurrencies that are supported by Coinbase. Before you go on to make your very first transaction, Coinbase provides you with the detailed fee structure and the total amount that will be deducted from your wallet.

Credit card option

Coinbase values user experience and has provided a more convenient way to buy cryptocurrency by making use of credit cards. Follow the steps below if you wish to buy cryptocurrency instantly by using your credit card:

Step 1: Go to your Coinbase account and click on the 'Buy/Sell' button at the top of the Dashboard page. After that, you will have to choose the 'Buy' option.

Step 2: Choose the cryptocurrency that you would like to buy; it's either Bitcoin or any other coin.

Step 3: In the payment section, select the credit card that you had previously verified.

Step 4: Enter the amount of cryptocurrency that you wish to buy and click on continue.

Step 5: Click on 'Buy Bitcoin instantly' and complete your payment. You will receive your cryptocurrency within 10 minutes when you use this method.

Though the credit card option makes it easy for anyone to buy cryptocurrency, it also has a higher processing fee which is equivalent to 3.99% of total cryptocurrency that you bought.

Are you not up for the volatility risks that come with Bitcoin anymore? Or maybe you just want to sell Bitcoin because you have gained a profit and need to cash it in? The process for selling your Bitcoin on the Coinbase exchange platform is very simple. Here I will break it down for you into a few easy steps:

Step 1: Log in to the homepage of your Coinbase account and click on the 'Buy/Sell' button.

Step 2: Choose the 'Sell' option and then the cryptocurrency that you wish to sell.

Step 3: Choose USD, GBP or Euro wallet to which money from the coin sale will be deposited.

Step 4: Enter the amount that you wish to sell.

Step 5: Before you confirm your sell order, you will be given a detailed breakdown of the fee structure which is the processing fee charged by the exchange. If everything looks all right, hit 'Sell Bitcoin instantly'. Your cryptocurrency will be converted to fiat currency and immediately reflected in your GBP, Euro or USD wallet.

You can then choose to transfer this amount to your bank account whenever you like. Don't forget to declare any profit you make on the sale to your relevant tax authority!

How to transfer Bitcoin with a cryptocurrency exchange

You can use the Coinbase wallet to carry out your frequent transactions such as online shopping or when dealing with other crypto enthusiasts. Sending and receiving coins on Coinbase is very simple. Just follow the steps below in order to make your first Bitcoin transaction.

Receiving Bitcoin:

Step 1: Go to the homepage of your Coinbase account and click on the 'Accounts' button.

Step 2: Choose the Bitcoin wallet and click on 'Receive' Bitcoin.

Step 3: Copy the Bitcoin wallet address that appears.

Step 4: Share this address with the person who needs to pay you. Once they transfer funds to this address, it will reflect in your wallet after it is confirmed on the Bitcoin network.

Remember, always send funds to the right wallet. If you end up sending Ethereum or any other cryptocurrency to a Bitcoin address then the funds will be lost forever.

Sending Bitcoin:

Step 1: Go to the homepage of your Coinbase account and click on the 'Accounts' button.

Step 2: Choose the Bitcoin wallet and click on 'Send' Bitcoin.

Step 3: On the screen that appears, enter the wallet address that you wish to transfer the Bitcoin to. After that enter the amount of Bitcoin.

Step 4: You then need to choose the fee that you would pay the miner to confirm your transaction. Then click on 'Continue'.

By choosing the priority transaction option, you can ensure that your transaction gets verified within the next 20 minutes. You can also choose the normal transaction fee if you wish to save some money and don't mind waiting for a longer time for your transaction to get verified. Transferring Bitcoin to another wallet or user varies between exchange platforms. Although every cryptocurrency exchange has a different set of instructions, they all seems to follow the same process.

Where to spend Bitcoin

At the beginning there was a pizza and that was all you could buy with Bitcoins! Nowadays, you can spend your Bitcoin on much more than Domino's pizza, in a wide variety of places, both online and offline. You are literally spoilt for choice.

Right from tipping to gift cards, paying for dinner to shopping, paying for your flights, furniture or gold, all of this is now possible. Even some musicians allow you to buy their albums using Bitcoins! You can pay for school or college, or even download movies and games using Bitcoin. There are a few legal and accounting firms that accept Bitcoin as payments too. The list is endless.

By now you should understand the practical aspects of buying, selling or transferring Bitcoin or any other cryptocurrency using the Coinbase crypto exchange.

Alternatively, you can use the same principle to make transactions on any other cryptocurrency exchange, depending on your geographical location. Do your research first and sign up with the most trusted local crypto exchange which offers excellent security features (for example, Kraken, Bittrex, Binance, Ploniex, KuCoin etc).

And of course, there is an important factor to consider when storing your Bitcoins in the wallet on the crypto exchange. The exchanges are holding your private keys and, thus you are not entirely in control of your funds.

That is something that you have to bear in mind from a security perspective. If you choose a reputed cryptocurrency exchange, then it shouldn't be an issue.

However, I would recommend storing your digital assets in your personal mobile or hardware crypto wallet. This enables you to have total control over your cryptocurrency funds.

Conclusion

This book was written for beginners who are interested in learning about the fundamentals of Bitcoin. This is an excellent starting point for readers that want to start with Bitcoin and cryptocurrencies. After reading this book, you should have a good understanding about the basic concept of cryptocurrency, Bitcoin and its blockchain technology. The book also covered interesting topics about the history of Bitcoin and its evolution. Moreover, it aimed to teach you how to start with Bitcoin and make your first investment in cryptocurrency. Finally, this comprehensive guide book explained in detail why Bitcoin has become a valuable asset and will reach its full potential in the near future.

Being an innovative blockchain-based technology, Bitcoin is creating new opportunities and revolutionizing the whole world. It is the first truly decentralized digital cryptocurrency that isn't dependent on any government or third-party institution. Hence, Bitcoin is set to replace banks and other centralized financial intermediaries and create better transparency in the global economy. In addition, Bitcoin has the potential to revolutionize the financial system, replace government-backed fiat currencies such as the US dollar and become the global digital currency.

Over the years, Bitcoin has increased in value tremendously and is on the way to establishing itself as 'digital gold'. Many crypto enthusiasts and financial experts see it as a better store of value than real gold. Even though Bitcoin is an extremely volatile asset, it is consistently outperforming other traditional assets like stocks, commodities or gold. Therefore, Bitcoin should definitely be considered as a profitable long-term investment asset that will reward its 'still early' investors with high returns in the future.

Many people are hesitant whether it is the right time to get involved with Bitcoin and consider investing in cryptocurrencies. Despite being in existence for ten years, Bitcoin is still at its early formation stage with less than ten million people involved in the cryptocurrency space. With three billion people on Earth with access to the Internet that still do not own any cryptocurrency, there is clearly some room for future growth.

This book has given a solid overview of Bitcoin fundamentals. By now, you should have learnt how Bitcoin works and fully understood the concept of this revolutionary technology.

Therefore, you are equipped with a good cryptocurrency knowledge and well prepared for an exciting journey in the cryptocurrency world that is full of potential investment opportunities!

Disclaimer

The information provided in this book doesn't constitute financial advice or investment recommendation. All content found in the book is for educational and informational purposes only. None of the content in the book should be relied upon for any investment activities. I strongly recommend that you perform your own independent research before making any investment decisions.

I express my own opinion in the book and do not offer, promote or encourage to buy, sell, or hold a
cryptocurrency or any other financial assets. Before engaging in such practices, every reader should consult a qualified financial advisor.

Bitcoin and other cryptocurrencies are an extremely volatile asset class. They are high risk investment and should always be treated with caution. Therefore, investing in cryptocurrencies has large potential rewards and also large potential risks. You must be aware of the risks and be willing to accept them. You should not purchase cryptocurrency unless you understand the extent of exposure to potential loss of the entire cryptocurrency investment. Before purchasing cryptocurrency, you must ensure that the nature, complexity and risks inherent in the investing in cryptocurrency are suitable for your objectives in light of your personal circumstances and financial position.

If you are considering investing in Bitcoin and other cryptocurrencies in a safer manner, always do your own research and educate yourself first. You must understand how the cryptocurrency environment works before investing your money.

Bibliography

Online recourses:

1.   https:// coinmarketcap.com: a website that contains the most comprehensive list of alternative coins, information and charts, the historical data and analysis of daily prices.

2.   htttps:// cointelegraph.com: a website that covers everything about Bitcoin in their latest news, prices, breakthroughs, and analysis, with emphasis on expert opinion and commentary from the crypto community.

3.   https:// coinnewstelegraph.com: a cryptocurrency coins news website which provides daily updates on Bitcoin and the cryptocurrency industry.

4.   https:// www.ccn.com: the most recent news outlet about the cryptocurrency industry, Bitcoin and blockchain which serves as a good source of information.

5.   https:// cryptopanic.com/news: a cryptocurrency news aggregator platform which collects daily updates on cryptocurrency from different mainstream media and helps the crypto community and traders to understand why price movements happens in the cryptocurrency market.

6.   https:// cryptogoat.net: cryptocurrency news aggregator platform indicating impact on Bitcoin and alternative coin prices and cryptocurrency market for traders and cryptocurrency enthusiasts.

7.   https:// www.coinna.com: cryptocurrency news aggregator platform that provides news information and data about cryptocurrencies and crypto exchanges.

8. http:// www.tradingview.com: an advanced financial visualization platform that provides charting software and technical analysis tools, the most active social network for traders and investors who share trading ideas and prices prediction. It also contains information and news updates on Bitcoin and cryptocurrencies.

9. https://www.thetimes03jan2009.com: Bitcoin Genesis Block newspaper.

10. https://qz.com/148399/ben-bernanke-bitcoin-may-hold-long-term-promise/ - Ben Bernanke's letter to Congress: Bitcoin and other virtual currencies "may hold long-term promise".

11. https://www.bitcoinblockhalf.com: Bitcoin block reward halving countdown page that provides statistical data on price, market capitalization and volume, and technical properties of Bitcoin network.

12. https://www.blockchain.com: is a Bitcoin block explorer service, as well as a cryptocurrency wallet provider. They also provide Bitcoin data charts, statistics and cryptocurrency market information.

13. https://www.forbes.com/crypto-blockchain/#6de0f0b12b6e: a global media page that features its original articles on technology, communication, politics and laws, science, and marketing topics. Forbes also reports related subjects such as finance, industry, investing, Bitcoin and blockchain.

14. http://historyofbitcoin.org: a timeline that illustrates Bitcoin development and its history from the very beginning all the way to present day.

15. https://woobull.com/why-hodl/: a web blog run by a crypto analyst and trader who provides an interactive chart for

cryptocurrency and price data analysis on crypto markets for investors.

16. https://cointelegraph.com/bitcoin-for-beginners/what-are-cryptocurrencies#how-to-buy.

17. https://cointelegraph.com/bitcoin-for-beginners/what-is-bitcoin#how-does-bitcoin-work.

18. https://en.bitcoinwiki.org/wiki/Cryptocurrency.

19. https://en.bitcoinwiki.org/wiki/Main_Page: a multilingual encyclopedia project on blockchain and cryptocurrency that contains over 6,000 articles about Bitcoin, Ethereum, crypto exchanges, history of cryptocurrency, mining.

20. https://en.bitcoinwiki.org/wiki/Buying_Bitcoin.

21. https:// www.investopedia.com: the world's leading source of financial content on the internet, ranging from market news to cryptocurrency related topics. The website serves as an educational recourse for investors.

22. https://www.bitcoin.org: the original domain used by the Bitcoin creator to announce Bitcoin, share the white paper, and distribute the code. It is maintained by Bitcoin developers and contains educational information on Bitcoin.

23. https://en.wikipedia.org/wiki/Satoshi_Nakamoto: a multilingual, online, free content encyclopedia that is created and edited by volunteers around the world.

24. https://en.bitcoinwiki.org/wiki/Satoshi_Nakamoto.

25. https://www.coindesk.com: a news website specializing in Bitcoin and digital currencies.

26. https://bitcoin.org/bitcoin.pdf: a pdf copy of bitcoin white paper explaining the concept of bitcoin technology.

27. https://www.cryptocurrencyguide.org/understanding-

blockchain-basics-and-use-cases/.

28.	https://www.cryptocurrencyguide.org/1-what-is-cryptocurrency/.

29.	https://nakamotoinstitute.org/literature/: a primary source of literature on cryptography and society, with a focus on the history and economics of Bitcoin.

Cryptocurrency Links & Information Resources:

1. https://alternative.me/crypto/fear-and-greed-index.
2. https://bitcointalk.org.
3. https://bittrex.com.
4. https://breakermag.com/the-bitcoin-white-paper-explained.
5. https://coinatmradar.com.
6. https://coinmarketcal.com.
7. https:// coinmarketcap.com.
8. https:// cointelegraph.com.
9. https:// coinnewstelegraph.com.
10. https://coin360.com.
11. https:// cryptogoat.net.
12. https:// cryptopanic.com.
13. https://cryptopotato.com.
14. https://cryptoprobe.net.
15. https://en.bitcoinwiki.org/wiki/Main_Page.
16. https://etherscan.io.
17. http://historyofbitcoin.org.
18. https://icowatchlist.com.
19. https://localbitcoins.com.
20. https://lightning.network.
21. https://nakamotoinstitute.org/literature.
22. https://1ml.com.
23. https://woobull.com/why-hodl.
24. https://www.binance.com.
25. https://walletgenerator.net.

26. https://www.bitaddress.org.

27. https://www.bitcoin.org.

28. https://www.bitcoinblockhalf.com.

29. https://www.bitmex.com.

30. https://www.blockchain.com.

31. https:// www.ccn.com.

32. https://www.coinbase.com.

33. https://www.coindesk.com.

34. https://www.coinigy.com.

35. https:// www.coinna.com.

36. https://www.cryptocompare.com.

37. https://www.easycrypto.nz.

38. https://www.forbes.com/crypto-blockchain.

39. https:// www.investopedia.com.

40. https://www.kraken.com.

41. https://www.litecoinblockhalf.com.

42. https://www.mycryptopedia.com.

43. https://www.newsbtc.com.

44. https://www.reddit.com/r/Bitcoin.

45. http:// www.tradingview.com.

Glossary

Altcoin – alternative cryptocurrency launched after Bitcoin.

AML (Anti Money Laundering) – refers to a set of procedures, laws, and regulations designed to stop the practice of generating income through illegal actions.

All-time high – the highest price that the coin has ever reached.

Bitcoin – a decentralized digital currency without a central bank or single administrator that can be sent from user to user on the peer-to-peer Bitcoin network without the need for intermediaries.

Bitcoin mining – a process of validating and adding transaction records to the Bitcoin's public ledger called the blockchain. It exists so that every transaction can be confirmed to the rest of the network, and every single user of the network can access this ledger. Running software on a computer that solves cryptographic mathematical problems and rewards miners with coins for solving the puzzle.

Block – all transaction data is permanently recorded in files called blocks. They can be thought of as the individual pages of the accounting ledger. Blocks are organized into a linear sequence over time known as the blockchain. New transactions are constantly being processed by miners into new blocks which are added to the end of the chain.

Blockchain – distributed public ledgers in which transactions made in

Bitcoin or another cryptocurrency are recorded chronologically and publicly. Hence, it is a decentralized public databases that everyone can access and read, but data on the blockchain can only be updated by the data owners. Data is then shared across thousands of computers who maintain the blockchain.

Cryptocurrency – a new kind of internet-based money that only exists digitally or virtually. It is an alternative digital form of payment that is designed to work as a medium of exchange for goods and services and transfer monetary value via the Internet.

Cryptocurrency Exchange – an online marketplace/ exchange platform where you can buy and sell cryptocurrencies.

Cryptocurrency wallet – a software program that stores private and public keys to interact with the various blockchains, used to securely store cryptocurrencies.

Cryptography – the process of converting text or numbers into code you can't break. It allows information to be kept secret and is safe. Cryptography is at the heart of the worldwide communication network today. It is a method of storing and transmitting data in a particular form so that only those for whom it is intended can read and process it. Bitcoin and other cryptocurrencies use cryptography everywhere, from its address system to its user experience, and even mining.

Initial Coin Offering – currently, there are many altcoins and tokens created by developers that are available in the digital market. The developers introduce a new digital cryptocurrency via a crowd sales method called

ICO. Initial Coin offering refers to the creation and sale of a certain amount of digital tokens.

Investment portfolio – a collection of investment assets held by an investment company, hedge fund, financial institution or individual.

Decentralized – a system or network without a single point of control.

Decentralization – the process by which the activities of an organization, particularly those regarding planning and decision making, are distributed or delegated away from a central, authoritative location or group.

Diversification – the process of allocating capital in a way that reduces the exposure to any one particular asset or risk. A common path towards diversification is to reduce risk or volatility by investing in a variety of assets.

Double spending – a fraudulent technique of spending the same amount twice.

Fiat – traditional money or currency that is a Government-issued Legal Tender such as USD or Euro.

Fork – related to the blockchain technology when an existing blockchain splits into two separate blockchains. Example: a single cryptocurrency is split into two different coins due to the change in the existing code, resulting in both an old and new version. Bitcoin Cash is a fork of original Bitcoin.

Halving – the 50% percent reduction in block rewards on the Bitcoin blockchain. Block reward is in the form of Bitcoins that are being awarded to Bitcoin miners.

Hardware wallet – a device that can securely store cryptocurrency. Hardware wallets are often regarded as the most secure way to hold a cryptocurrency. Ledger Nano S and Trezor – two of the most popular hardware wallets.

Hash – a hash algorithm turns a large amount of data into a fixed-length hash (a string of characters that acts as a cryptographic key). The same hash will always result from the same data, but modifying the data in any way will completely change the hash. In cryptography most data is encrypted using hash algorithms, they are at the core of cryptocurrency tokens and blockchains. Bitcoin specifically uses SHA-256, SHA stands for Secure Hash Algorithm.

Hash Power – the rate at which a given piece of hardware can mine a coin (mining is the cracking of cryptographic codes). It is like horsepower but refers to how fast
hardware can decrypt hashes.

KYC (Know Your Customer) – the process of a business verifying the identity of its clients and assessing potential risks of illegal intentions for the business relationship.

Market capitalization – total market value of the volume of available cryptocurrencies multiplied by its price per unit of currency.

Miners – mining activities are carried out by a special group of people called miners. Miners solve
computational puzzles which allow them to chain together blocks of transactions. Because their role is to secure the network and process transactions, as a reward they receive new Bitcoins and transaction fees. Miners get rewards for their service every 10 minutes.

Nodes – any computer that hosts the blockchain. The blockchain isn't stored in one place and is distributed, each node running it plays an important role in verifying the transactions on the ledger.

Proof-of-Work – an economic measure protocol that has the main goal to deter denial of service attacks and other service abuses on the blockchain. Proof of work describes the process that allows the Bitcoin network to remain robust by making the process of mining, or recording transactions, difficult. Proof-of-Work (PoW) was originally invented as a measure against email spams. Only later it was adapted to be used in digital cash.

Proof-of-Stake – a type of algorithm by which a cryptocurrency blockchain network aims to achieve distributed consensus in choosing the creator of the next block. Proof of Stake (PoS) concept states that a person can mine or validate block transactions according to how many coins he or she holds.

Satoshi – one hundred millionth of a Bitcoin, the smallest denomination of Bitcoin.

Satoshi Nakamoto – a persona created by the person or community of people who created Bitcoin. Satoshi may or may not exist and may or may not be alive. He/she sacrificed fame (and potentially a fortune) to remain anonymous.

Scalability – the maximum amount of transactions the bitcoin payment network can process.

Volatility – measures the degree of variation of market prices over time. This means that the price of Bitcoin can change dramatically over a short time period in either direction. It refers to the amount of uncertainty or risk related to the size of changes in Bitcoin value. More volatile assets are considered riskier than less volatile assets because the price is expected to be less predictable.

White paper – an informational document that is designed to help the reader to understand the technical details, the purpose, and development of the cryptocurrency project.

www.ingramcontent.com/pod-product-compliance
Lightning Source LLC
Chambersburg PA
CBHW071208050326
40689CB00011B/2275